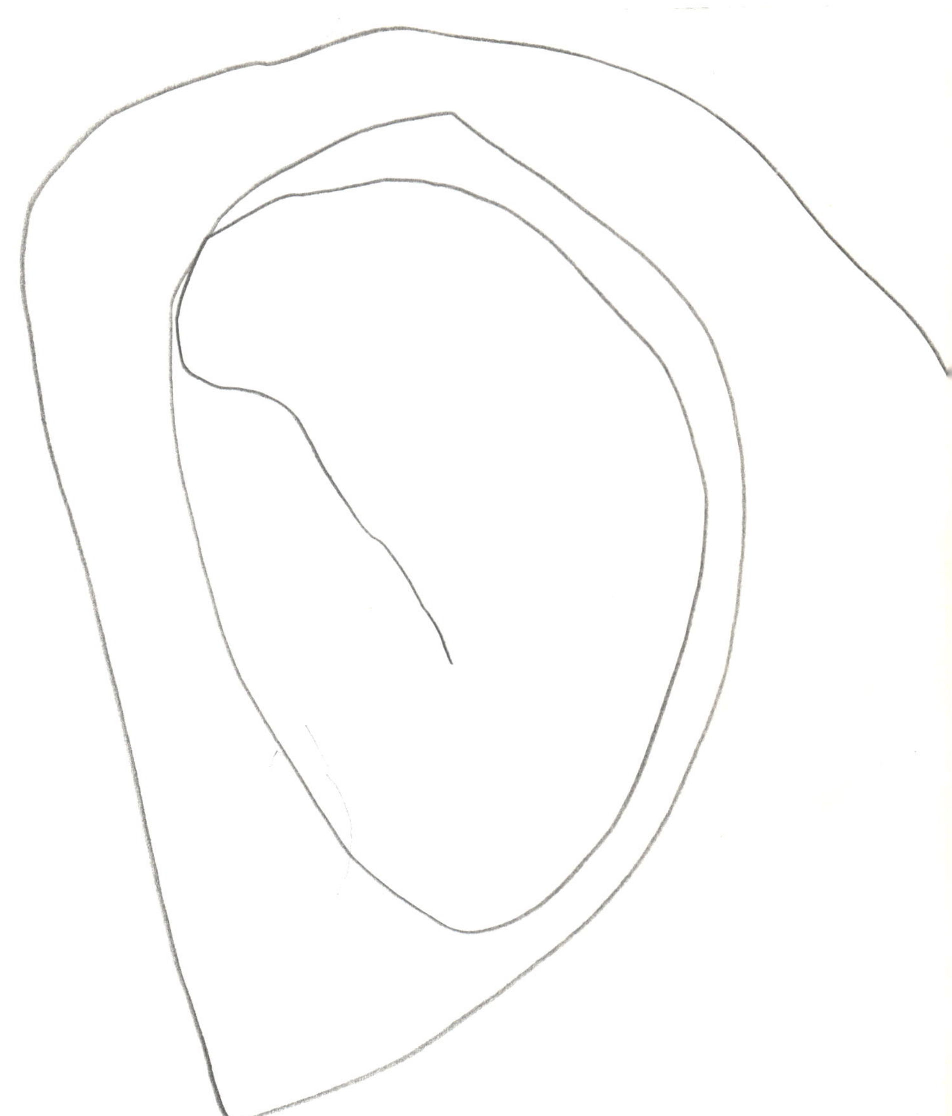

KNOW YOUR GOVERNMENT

The U.S. Fish and Wildlife Service

KNOW YOUR GOVERNMENT

The U.S. Fish and Wildlife Service

Eric Jay Dolin

CHELSEA HOUSE PUBLISHERS

CHELSEA HOUSE PUBLISHERS
Editor-in-Chief: Nancy Toff
Executive Editor: Remmel T. Nunn
Managing Editor: Karyn Gullen Browne
Copy Chief: Juliann Barbato
Picture Editor: Adrian G. Allen
Art Director: Maria Epes
Manufacturing Manager: Gerald Levine

Know Your Government
Senior Editor: Kathy Kuhtz

Staff for **THE U.S. FISH AND WILDLIFE SERVICE**
Assistant Editor: Gillian Bucky
Copy Editor: Nicole Bowen
Deputy Copy Chief: Ellen Scordato
Editorial Assistant: Elizabeth Nix
Picture Researcher: Ed Dixon
Assistant Art Director: Laurie Jewell
Senior Designer: Noreen M. Lamb
Production Coordinator: Joseph Romano

First Printing

1 3 5 7 9 8 6 4 2

Library of Congress Cataloging-in-Publication Data
Dolin, Eric Jay.
The U.S. Fish and Wildlife Service.
(Know your government)
Bibliography: p.
Includes index.
Summary: Surveys the history of the United States Fish and Wildlife Service, describing its structure, current function, and influence on American society.
1. United States. Fish and Wildlife Service—Juvenile literature. [1. United States. Fish and Wildlife Service. 2. Wildlife conservation] I. Title. II. Series: Know your government (New York, N.Y.)
SK361.D65 1989 353.0082′36 88-25818
1-55546-128-X
0-7910-0878-9 (pbk.)

CONTENTS

KNOW YOUR GOVERNMENT

THE AMERICAN RED CROSS
THE BUREAU OF INDIAN AFFAIRS
THE CENTRAL INTELLIGENCE AGENCY
THE COMMISSION ON CIVIL RIGHTS
THE DEPARTMENT OF AGRICULTURE
THE DEPARTMENT OF THE AIR FORCE
THE DEPARTMENT OF THE ARMY
THE DEPARTMENT OF COMMERCE
THE DEPARTMENT OF DEFENSE
THE DEPARTMENT OF EDUCATION
THE DEPARTMENT OF ENERGY
THE DEPARTMENT OF HEALTH AND HUMAN SERVICES
THE DEPARTMENT OF HOUSING AND URBAN DEVELOPMENT
THE DEPARTMENT OF THE INTERIOR
THE DEPARTMENT OF JUSTICE
THE DEPARTMENT OF LABOR
THE DEPARTMENT OF THE NAVY
THE DEPARTMENT OF STATE
THE DEPARTMENT OF TRANSPORTATION
THE DEPARTMENT OF THE TREASURY
THE DRUG ENFORCEMENT ADMINISTRATION
THE ENVIRONMENTAL PROTECTION AGENCY
THE EQUAL EMPLOYMENT OPPORTUNITIES COMMISSION
THE FEDERAL AVIATION ADMINISTRATION
THE FEDERAL BUREAU OF INVESTIGATION
THE FEDERAL COMMUNICATIONS COMMISSION
THE FEDERAL GOVERNMENT: HOW IT WORKS
THE FEDERAL RESERVE SYSTEM
THE FEDERAL TRADE COMMISSION
THE FOOD AND DRUG ADMINISTRATION
THE FOREST SERVICE
THE HOUSE OF REPRESENTATIVES
THE IMMIGRATION AND NATURALIZATION SERVICE
THE INTERNAL REVENUE SERVICE
THE LIBRARY OF CONGRESS
THE NATIONAL AERONAUTICS AND SPACE ADMINISTRATION
THE NATIONAL ARCHIVES AND RECORDS ADMINISTRATION
THE NATIONAL FOUNDATION ON THE ARTS AND HUMANITIES
THE NATIONAL PARK SERVICE
THE NATIONAL SCIENCE FOUNDATION
THE NUCLEAR REGULATORY COMMISSION
THE PEACE CORPS
THE PRESIDENCY
THE PUBLIC HEALTH SERVICE
THE SECURITIES AND EXCHANGE COMMISSION
THE SENATE
THE SMALL BUSINESS ADMINISTRATION
THE SMITHSONIAN
THE SUPREME COURT
THE TENNESSEE VALLEY AUTHORITY
THE U.S. ARMS CONTROL AND DISARMAMENT AGENCY
THE U.S. COAST GUARD
THE U.S. CONSTITUTION
THE U.S. FISH AND WILDLIFE SERVICE
THE U.S. INFORMATION AGENCY
THE U.S. MARINE CORPS
THE U.S. MINT
THE U.S. POSTAL SERVICE
THE U.S. SECRET SERVICE
THE VETERANS ADMINISTRATION

CHELSEA HOUSE PUBLISHERS

INTRODUCTION

Government: Crises of Confidence

Arthur M. Schlesinger, jr.

From the start, Americans have regarded their government with a mixture of reliance and mistrust. The men who founded the republic did not doubt the indispensability of government. "If men were angels," observed the 51st Federalist Paper, "no government would be necessary." But men are not angels. Because human beings are subject to wicked as well as to noble impulses, government was deemed essential to assure freedom and order.

At the same time, the American revolutionaries knew that government could also become a source of injury and oppression. The men who gathered in Philadelphia in 1787 to write the Constitution therefore had two purposes in mind. They wanted to establish a strong central authority and to limit that central authority's capacity to abuse its power.

To prevent the abuse of power, the Founding Fathers wrote two basic principles into the new Constitution. The principle of federalism divided power between the state governments and the central authority. The principle of the separation of powers subdivided the central authority itself into three branches—the executive, the legislative, and the judiciary—so that "each may be a check on the other." The *Know Your Government* series focuses on the major executive departments and agencies in these branches of the federal government.

The Constitution did not plan the executive branch in any detail. After vesting the executive power in the president, it assumed the existence of "executive departments" without specifying what these departments should be. Congress began defining their functions in 1789 by creating the Departments of State, Treasury, and War. The secretaries in charge of these departments made up President Washington's first cabinet. Congress also provided for a legal officer, and President Washington soon invited the attorney general, as he was called, to attend cabinet meetings. As need required, Congress created more executive departments.

Setting up the cabinet was only the first step in organizing the American state. With almost no guidance from the Constitution, President Washington, seconded by Alexander Hamilton, his brilliant secretary of the treasury, equipped the infant republic with a working administrative structure. The Federalists believed in both executive energy and executive accountability and set high standards for public appointments. The Jeffersonian opposition had less faith in strong government and preferred local government to the central authority. But when Jefferson himself became president in 1801, although he set out to change the direction of policy, he found no reason to alter the framework the Federalists had erected.

By 1801 there were about 3,000 federal civilian employees in a nation of a little more than 5 million people. Growth in territory and population steadily enlarged national responsibilities. Thirty years later, when Jackson was president, there were more than 11,000 government workers in a nation of 13 million. The federal establishment was increasing at a faster rate than the population.

Jackson's presidency brought significant changes in the federal service. He believed that the executive branch contained too many officials who saw their jobs as "species of property" and as "a means of promoting individual interest." Against the idea of a permanent service based on life tenure, Jackson argued for the periodic redistribution of federal offices, contending that this was the democratic way and that official duties could be made "so plain and simple that men of intelligence may readily qualify themselves for their performance." He called this policy rotation-in-office. His opponents called it the spoils system.

In fact, partisan legend exaggerated the extent of Jackson's removals. More than 80 percent of federal officeholders retained their jobs. Jackson discharged no larger a proportion of government workers than Jefferson had done a generation earlier. But the rise in these years of mass political parties gave federal patronage new importance as a means of building the party and of rewarding activists. Jackson's successors were less restrained in the distribution of spoils. As the federal establishment grew—to nearly 40,000 by 1861—the politicization of the public service excited increasing concern.

After the Civil War the spoils system became a major political issue. High-minded men condemned it as the root of all political evil. The spoilsmen, said the British commentator James Bryce, "have distorted and depraved the mechanism of politics." Patronage, by giving jobs to unqualified, incompetent, and dishonest persons, lowered the standards of public service and nourished corrupt political machines. Office-seekers pursued presidents and cabinet secretaries without mercy. "Patronage," said Ulysses S. Grant after his presidency, "is the bane of the presidential office." "Every time I appoint someone to office," said another political leader, "I make a hundred enemies and one ingrate." George William Curtis, the president of the National Civil Service Reform League, summed up the indictment. He said,

> The theory which perverts public trusts into party spoils, making public employment dependent upon personal favor and not on proved merit, necessarily ruins the self-respect of public employees, destroys the function of party in a republic, prostitutes elections into a desperate strife for personal profit, and degrades the national character by lowering the moral tone and standard of the country.

The object of civil service reform was to promote efficiency and honesty in the public service and to bring about the ethical regeneration of public life. Over bitter opposition from politicians, the reformers in 1883 passed the Pendleton Act, establishing a bipartisan Civil Service Commission, competitive examinations, and appointment on merit. The Pendleton Act also gave the president authority to extend by executive order the number of "classified" jobs—that is, jobs subject to the merit system. The act applied initially only to about 14,000 of the more than 100,000 federal positions. But by the end of the 19th century 40 percent of federal jobs had moved into the classified category.

Civil service reform was in part a response to the growing complexity of American life. As society grew more organized and problems more technical, official duties were no longer so plain and simple that any person of intelligence could perform them. In public service, as in other areas, the all-round man was yielding ground to the expert, the amateur to the professional. The excesses of the spoils system thus provoked the counter-ideal of scientific public administration, separate from politics and, as far as possible, insulated against it.

The cult of the expert, however, had its own excesses. The idea that administration could be divorced from policy was an illusion. And in the realm of policy, the expert, however much segregated from partisan politics, can never attain perfect objectivity. He remains the prisoner of his own set of values. It is these values rather than technical expertise that determine fundamental judgments of public policy. To turn over such judgments to experts, moreover, would be to abandon democracy itself; for in a democracy final decisions must be made by the people and their elected representatives. "The business of the expert," the British political scientist Harold Laski rightly said, "is to be on tap and not on top."

Politics, however, were deeply ingrained in American folkways. This meant intermittent tension between the presidential government, elected every four years by the people, and the permanent government, which saw presidents come and go while it went on forever. Sometimes the permanent government knew better than its political masters; sometimes it opposed or sabotaged valuable new initiatives. In the end a strong president with effective cabinet secretaries could make the permanent government responsive to presidential purpose, but it was often an exasperating struggle.

The struggle within the executive branch was less important, however, than the growing impatience with bureaucracy in society as a whole. The 20th century saw a considerable expansion of the federal establishment. The Great Depression and the New Deal led the national government to take on a variety of new responsibilities. The New Deal extended the federal regulatory apparatus. By 1940, in a nation of 130 million people, the number of federal workers for the first time passed the 1 million mark. The Second World War brought federal civilian employment to 3.8 million in 1945. With peace, the federal establishment declined to around 2 million by 1950. Then growth resumed, reaching 2.8 million by the 1980s.

The New Deal years saw rising criticism of "big government" and "bureaucracy." Businessmen resented federal regulation. Conservatives worried about the impact of paternalistic government on individual self-reliance, on community responsibility, and on economic and personal freedom. The nation in effect renewed the old debate between Hamilton and Jefferson in the early republic, although with an ironic exchange of positions. For the Hamiltonian constituency, the "rich and well-born," once the advocate of affirmative government, now condemned government intervention, while the Jeffersonian constituency, the plain people, once the advocate of a weak central government and of states' rights, now favored government intervention.

In the 1980s, with the presidency of Ronald Reagan, the debate has burst out with unusual intensity. According to conservatives, government intervention abridges liberty, stifles enterprise, and is inefficient, wasteful, and arbitrary. It disturbs the harmony of the self-adjusting market and creates worse troubles than it solves. Get government off our backs, according to the popular cliché, and our problems will solve themselves. When government is necessary, let it be at the local level, close to the people. Above all, stop the inexorable growth of the federal government.

In fact, for all the talk about the "swollen" and "bloated" bureaucracy, the federal establishment has not been growing as inexorably as many Americans seem to believe. In 1949, it consisted of 2.1 million people. Thirty years later, while the country had grown by 70 million, the federal force had grown only by 750,000. Federal workers were a smaller percentage of the population in 1985 than they were in 1955—or in 1940. The federal establishment, in short, has not kept pace with population growth. Moreover, national defense and the postal service account for 60 percent of federal employment.

Why then the widespread idea about the remorseless growth of government? It is partly because in the 1960s the national government assumed new and intrusive functions: affirmative action in civil rights, environmental protection, safety and health in the workplace, community organization, legal aid to the poor. Although this enlargement of the federal regulatory role was accompanied by marked growth in the size of government on all levels, the expansion has taken place primarily in state and local government. Whereas the federal force increased by only 27 percent in the 30 years after 1950, the state and local government force increased by an astonishing 212 percent.

Despite the statistics, the conviction flourishes in some minds that the national government is a steadily growing behemoth swallowing up the liberties of the people. The foes of Washington prefer local government, feeling it is closer to the people and therefore allegedly more responsive to popular needs. Obviously there is a great deal to be said for settling local questions locally. But local government is characteristically the government of the locally powerful. Historically, the way the locally powerless have won their human and constitutional rights has often been through appeal to the national government. The national government has vindicated racial justice against local bigotry, defended the Bill of Rights against local vigilantism, and protected natural resources against local greed. It has civilized industry and secured the rights of labor organizations. Had the states' rights creed prevailed, there would perhaps still be slavery in the United States.

The national authority, far from diminishing the individual, has given most Americans more personal dignity and liberty than ever before. The individual freedoms destroyed by the increase in national authority have been in the main the freedom to deny black Americans their rights as citizens; the freedom to put small children to work in mills and immigrants in sweatshops; the freedom to pay starvation wages, require barbarous working hours, and permit squalid working conditions; the freedom to deceive in the sale of goods and securities; the freedom to pollute the environment—all freedoms that, one supposes, a civilized nation can readily do without.

"Statements are made," said President John F. Kennedy in 1963, "labelling the Federal Government an outsider, an intruder, an adversary. . . . The United States Government is not a stranger or not an enemy. It is the people of fifty states joining in a national effort. . . . Only a great national effort by a great people working together can explore the mysteries of space, harvest the products at the bottom of the ocean, and mobilize the human, natural, and material resources of our lands."

So an old debate continues. However, Americans are of two minds. When pollsters ask large, spacious questions—Do you think government has become too involved in your lives? Do you think government should stop regulating business?—a sizable majority opposes big government. But when asked specific questions about the practical work of government—Do you favor social security? unemployment compensation? Medicare? health and safety standards in factories? environmental protection? government guarantee of jobs for everyone seeking employment? price and wage controls when inflation threatens?—a sizable majority approves of intervention.

In general, Americans do not want less government. What they want is more efficient government. They want government to do a better job. For a time in the 1970s, with Vietnam and Watergate, Americans lost confidence in the national government. In 1964, more than three-quarters of those polled had thought the national government could be trusted to do right most of the time. By 1980 only one-quarter was prepared to offer such trust. But by 1984 trust in the federal government to manage national affairs had climbed back to 45 percent.

Bureaucracy is a term of abuse. But it is impossible to run any large organization, whether public or private, without a bureaucracy's division of labor and hierarchy of authority. And we live in a world of large organizations. Without bureaucracy modern society would collapse. The problem is not to abolish bureaucracy, but to make it flexible, efficient, and capable of innovation.

Two hundred years after the drafting of the Constitution, Americans still regard government with a mixture of reliance and mistrust—a good combination. Mistrust is the best way to keep government reliable. Informed criticism is the means of correcting governmental inefficiency, incompetence, and arbitrariness; that is, of best enabling government to play its essential role. For without government, we cannot attain the goals of the Founding Fathers. Without an understanding of government, we cannot have the informed criticism that makes government do the job right. It is the duty of every American citizen to know our government—which is what this series is all about.

The bald eagle, America's national bird, is one of the nearly 500 endangered native animal species protected by the U.S. Fish and Wildlife Service. Carrying out endangered species legislation is one of the service's most important responsibilities.

ONE

To Benefit a Nation

The United States Fish and Wildlife Service (USFWS) is in charge of conserving, protecting, and enhancing the nation's fish and wildlife and their habitats. The largest agency of its kind in the world, the USFWS employs more than 6,400 people at its headquarters in Washington, D.C., and in offices throughout the country and has an annual budget of more than $700 million.

Unlike many other federal agencies, the USFWS does not have an organic act—which means, simply, that no one piece of legislation established the USFWS and defined its powers. Instead, today's USFWS inherited its duties from a series of federal agencies established to promote more efficient and commercially sound fish and wildlife management. The federal government first became involved in the management and protection of fish and wildlife in 1871, when Congress established the U.S. Fish Commission to study shrinking food-fish populations. In 1886, Congress formed the Division of Economic Ornithology and Mammalogy to study ways to protect agricultural crops and livestock from destructive pests and predators. (Ornithology is a branch of zoology that deals with birds, whereas mammalogy deals with mammals.)

Over the years, the focuses and responsibilities of these two agencies changed to encompass broader fish and wildlife protection to benefit not only

Fishing for bass on the Potomac River. The USFWS has long maintained fisheries throughout the nation for recreational and commercial use.

commercial interests but sport and recreational users of fish and wildlife as well. The agencies supervised federal efforts in numerous areas, including scientific studies of animal populations and research on the damaging effects of human activities on wildlife; predator control; the establishment of national wildlife refuges; the protection of migratory birds and endangered species; and the restoration of various fish and wildlife populations. In 1903, the U.S. Fish Commission was renamed the Bureau of Fisheries; the Division of Economic Ornithology and Mammalogy was redesignated the Division of Biological Survey in 1896 and then the Bureau of Biological Survey in 1905. The two bureaus were later combined through a series of reorganizations; in 1956, their responsibilities were given to the newly created U.S. Fish and Wildlife Service.

Today's USFWS has diverse responsibilities that include managing hundreds of wildlife refuges; protecting migratory birds, endangered species, and marine mammals; conducting research to prevent animal diseases; and enforcing federal fish and wildlife laws. In addition, the USFWS advises other federal agencies on ways in which they can avoid harming fish and wildlife while carrying out their responsibilities. The service also assists state and foreign governments in managing their fish and wildlife resources by giving them both technical and financial assistance. Together, these activities play an important role in protecting, conserving, and restoring the natural environment.

The natural environment is not the only beneficiary of the USFWS's activities, however. By protecting wild animals in their natural habitat, the USFWS is also advancing the public's opportunity to enjoy nature—to hike through a national wildlife refuge, watch an eagle soar, or fish in a freshwater lake. Through its varied responsibilities and the nature of its relationship with the public, other federal agencies, Congress, and the states, the USFWS plays an essential role in fish and wildlife management and in the preservation of our natural environment for the benefit of all Americans.

A flock of snow geese lands in a barley field. In the 19th century, thousands of Americans moved into formerly unpopulated areas and built homes and businesses that threatened to overwhelm the natural habitat of these and other birds and animals.

TWO

The USFWS Predecessors

When the first European colonists arrived in North America in the 1600s, they found an abundance of wildlife. The lakes, rivers, and coastal waters were teeming with trout, bass, cod, and salmon. In the woods and fields were deer, rabbits, turkeys, and pheasant. These wildlife resources were so plentiful that the colonists believed they could not exhaust the supply. But as the colonies—and soon the United States—expanded during the 1600s, 1700s, and early 1800s, so too grew the need for food to feed the population. An increasing amount of wildlife had to be hunted and killed to support this growth.

Hunting and fishing were not the settlers' only activities that threatened native species of wildlife. The expansion of settled territory brought with it a corresponding decrease in the area of natural habitat, on which wildlife depends. The construction of towns, farms, and roads all required that forests be cleared away and, with them, the wildlife found there. In addition, the refuse produced by new population centers was often harmful to wildlife. For example, sewage discharged into a river could destroy fish and shellfish or make them unhealthy to eat. By the late 1800s, it had become clear that the nation's wildlife resources were not infinitely abundant, and that human activity could decimate entire species.

Only preserved specimens remain of the passenger pigeon, a once-abundant species of North American bird. Human activity—in this case, hunting for pleasure and profit—caused the species to become extinct by the early 20th century.

One classic example of human destruction of an animal species is the story of the passenger pigeon. At the beginning of the 19th century, there were nearly 5 billion passenger pigeons in North America, making it the most common bird on the continent. Tasty and easy to kill, the passenger pigeon was valuable as a source of food for both humans and animals. The enthusiasm with which sport and commercial hunters pursued the bird was so great that passenger pigeons became scarce by the end of the 19th century. In 1914, the last passenger pigeon, named Martha, died in Ohio in the Cincinnati Zoo.

Similarly, millions of buffalo were slaughtered by sport hunters who shot the mighty beasts from the windows of trains traveling across the western plains of the United States. Others hunted buffalo for their hides, which were used to make leather for warm overcoats and other products. Between 1872 and 1874 more than 3 million buffalo were killed annually for their hides. Faced with attacks by sport hunters and a strong demand for leather, the buffalo population declined precipitously. In 1867, an estimated 13 million buffalo roamed the ranges in the western states; by 1883 just 200 were left. Only through the intervention of dedicated conservationists and Congress did the buffalo avoid the fate of the passenger pigeon. For example, in 1909, Congress authorized the purchase of 12,000 acres in Montana as a refuge for the remaining buffalo.

The desire for buffalo overcoats was not the only fashion trend that proved disastrous to wildlife. Exotic bird feathers were a favorite decoration for women's hats in the late 19th century. Millions of birds, such as herons and egrets, were shot and plucked to satisfy the demand for feathers. In 1886, the American Ornithologists' Union, one of the earliest wildlife-conservation organizations, estimated that 5 million birds were being killed annually for this purpose. One hunter set a record by killing 141,000 birds in one season; this figure is especially disturbing because, in many cases, only one part of the bird—such as a beautiful mating plume—was considered of value. Thus, once the hunter got what he was after, the rest of the bird was left in the field to rot.

As the populations of certain animal species declined, concerned citizens established private organizations dedicated to conserving America's wildlife

Railroad passengers take aim at a herd of buffalo as their train speeds westward. Shooting buffalo in this manner was a popular sport in the mid-19th century and resulted in the near-extinction of the species.

A late 19th-century bird-study class, conducted under the auspices of the Audubon Society, one of the nation's first wildlife conservation organizations.

resources. The American Ornithologists' Union was formed in 1883 and the Audubon Society (named after ornithologist John James Audubon) in 1886. (In 1905, various state Audubon societies merged to form the National Audubon Society.) States became involved in wildlife conservation as well. In 1850, New Jersey passed legislation to prevent the killing of various small and harmless birds. In 1865, Massachusetts created the first state fish and wildlife agency; many other states soon followed suit. By 1880, all of the states had laws primarily designed to protect wildlife.

In addition to recognizing the destructive impact of human activity on wildlife populations, Americans in the latter part of the 19th century acquired a heightened understanding of wildlife's impact on agriculture. Scientists and naturalists knew that certain species of wildlife could improve agricultural yield. For example, many species of birds ate insects that fed on and often destroyed crops; thus, by decreasing the number of insects, birds helped the farmer grow more food. On the other hand, it was also clear that some wildlife species could reduce agricultural productivity. For example, coyotes and wolves were known to kill livestock, including sheep, cattle, and chickens.

In response to national concern about the depletion of wildlife and wildlife's relationship to agriculture, Congress brought the federal government into the area of wildlife management by creating two organizations: the United States Fish Commission, formed in 1871, and the Division of Economic Ornithology and Mammalogy, formed in 1886.

The U.S. Fish Commission

The United States Fish Commission was created on February 9, 1871, and charged with studying populations of commercial food fishes of the inland and coastal waters of the United States and recommending ways to protect threatened fisheries. After the commission's initial investigations found certain fish populations to be in decline, Congress expanded the commission's activities to include breeding and distributing freshwater fish and eggs nationwide. Congress created the first federal fish hatchery on California's McCloud River in 1872 for the purpose of breeding salmon, whose populations in the northwestern United States were shrinking rapidly, and soon established hatcheries in other parts of the country. These federal efforts, along with similar efforts by states and individuals, helped to stem the decline of many fish populations.

Fish cannery workers in the Pacific Northwest. Soon after the U.S. Fish Commission was formed in 1871, it began studying new methods for processing and storing fish.

Over the next few decades, the Fish Commission gained added responsibilities. In 1879, Congress ordered the commission to collect and publish statistics on the commercial fishing industry (for example, the size of the annual catch). Shortly thereafter, the commission became involved in investigating techniques for storing and processing fish, evaluating the potential of offshore fishing areas, and developing improved fishing gear and methods. By the late 1890s, the commission was also investigating populations of seals—which were hunted for their fur—and conducting fish surveys in Alaska. The commission's Alaska work expanded in subsequent years to include regulating salmon and other fisheries, studying the habits of commercial migratory fish, and collecting statistics on the amount of fish that was canned.

On February 14, 1903, by an act of Congress, the U.S. Fish Commission was renamed the Bureau of Fisheries and incorporated into the newly created Department of Commerce and Labor. Congress placed the bureau in this new department because its primary goal was commerce related: It supported and promoted the development of the commercial fishing industry. (This is also the

Seals line a beach in Alaska. The U.S. Fish Commission collected data on seal populations, which were threatened by hunters in pursuit of seal fur.

Workers manually open the floodgates of a dam in Nevada in the early 20th century. Because dams blocked the path of a river, they posed a threat to anadromous fish—species that must travel upstream to reproduce.

reason the Bureau of Fisheries was placed in the Department of Commerce when the Department of Commerce and Labor divided in 1913.)

In the early part of the 20th century, the federal government began sponsoring the construction of dams throughout the western United States. At first, these dams were used to irrigate parts of the arid West for agricultural purposes; later, they were also used to generate hydroelectric power, to control floods, and to provide recreational areas. However, not all the effects of these dams were beneficial. Some fish populations whose habitats were severely altered as a result of damming suffered sharp declines. Hardest hit were the *anadromous* fish, which spend the majority of their lifetime in the ocean but migrate upstream to spawn (reproduce) in freshwater. Dams often made it impossible for such fish to ascend the rivers.

Soon after the federal government began sponsoring dam construction, legislators became concerned about the danger posed by the dams to fish populations. As a result, Congress passed the Federal Water Power Act of 1920, authorizing the secretary of commerce to recommend that federally sponsored dams include devices that would enable fish to swim around the dam. These devices are commonly referred to as *fish ladders*. Fourteen years

The salmon, an anadromous fish, was particularly threatened by the damming of rivers in the Northwest. Legislation in the early part of the 20th century enabled the Bureau of Fisheries to press companies building dams to install fish ladders in dam facilities.

later, Congress once again addressed the issue of protecting fish in dammed rivers in the Fish and Wildlife Coordination Act of 1934, legislation passed to promote wildlife conservation and rehabilitation. Specifically, the act required all federal agencies to consult with the Bureau of Fisheries before constructing a dam or issuing a license for dam construction to determine if fish ladders should be included as part of the dam. But although the Fish and Wildlife Coordination Act further enabled the bureau to protect fish in dammed rivers, its power was still limited: Even if the bureau concluded that a dam should have a fish ladder, it was up to the dam construction or licensing agency to decide whether or not to accept the bureau's decision.

The review of dam projects was only one aspect of the Fish and Wildlife Coordination Act that affected fish. Other provisions authorized the bureau to aid the states in stocking fisheries, to research the effects of pollution on fish, and to conduct surveys of fish in federally owned waters. The act also allowed the bureau to use the impounded waters (any waters confined as a result of damming) of any federally sponsored dam for raising fish.

In the late 1930s, Congress once again took up the issue of protecting fish populations on dammed rivers. This time, however, their concern was quite specific—to restore the Pacific salmon and steelhead trout in the Columbia River basin of the upper northwestern United States (Washington, Oregon, and Idaho). Vast numbers of these fish had once supported a thriving commercial fishing industry, but their populations had declined as more dams were built on the basin's rivers in the early part of the 20th century. The dams were especially damaging because these two species of fish are anadromous. To improve conditions for these fish, Congress passed the Mitchell Act of 1938. This act authorized the Bureau of Fisheries to construct fish ladders and other structures that would aid in fish migration, to conduct fish surveys, to improve feeding and spawning habitats, and to establish salmon hatcheries in Washington, Oregon, and Idaho to be used in restocking the basin.

Two salmon lie trapped in a fence at a fish hatchery in Oregon. The 1938 Mitchell Act authorized the Bureau of Fisheries to maintain salmon hatcheries in Washington, Oregon, and Idaho for the purpose of replenishing the depleted salmon population of the Columbia River basin.

By the end of the 1930s, the federal government could look back on a number of accomplishments in the area of fish management and protection. As a result of the passage of various laws, more was known about the status of certain commercial fish populations and efforts were being made to reverse population declines where they were found. In addition, the Bureau of Fisheries had been authorized to protect fish populations threatened by dam building. However, fish were not the only natural resource that the federal government was concerned about during the late 19th and early 20th centuries. Wildlife, too, came increasingly under the control of the government during that period. The first federal action with regard to wildlife protection was the creation of the Division of Economic Ornithology and Mammalogy.

The Division of Economic Ornithology and Mammalogy

The Division of Economic Ornithology and Mammalogy was created by Congress on June 30, 1886, and placed within the Department of Agriculture. The division's initial responsibility was primarily economic: to educate farmers about ways to save money by protecting their crops and livestock from pests and predators. Over the next 10 years the division's responsibilities changed, and by 1896 its primary activities were scientific. Foremost among these activities were extensive surveys that resulted in maps showing the distribution of wildlife and plants throughout the country. As a consequence of the division's shift in emphasis, Congress renamed it the Division of Biological Survey on April 25, 1896.

The division's surveying and mapping activities later expanded not only throughout the United States but beyond the country's continental borders to Alaska, Canada, and Mexico. The Alaska territory, purchased by the United States in 1867 for $7 million, remained largely uninhabited and unexplored until later in the 19th century. However, with the discovery of gold in Alaska and in the neighboring Canadian territory in the late 1890s, thousands of people headed north to find their fortunes. The Division of Biological Survey was also curious about the Alaskan wilderness and in 1899 began conducting surveys and preparing maps of Alaskan animal and plant life. One year later, on behalf of the United States, the division entered into an agreement with Canada to coordinate surveying and mapping efforts designed to identify the species inhabiting the border areas between the two countries. The division soon reached a similar agreement with Mexico.

Two men set a bear trap in the late 19th century. Bears and other wild animals often attacked livestock and caused farmers to suffer economic losses, particularly in the western states.

Around the turn of the century, the public and Congress began to voice objections to the division's predominantly scientific focus. Although many people felt that the survey and mapping work was valuable, they wanted the division to become more involved in work that would directly benefit humans. This sentiment resulted in a series of congressional and presidential actions that radically altered the division's activities and responsibilities. From March 3, 1905, when the Division of Biological Survey was renamed the Bureau of Biological Survey, until 1940, when it was incorporated into the newly created Fish and Wildlife Service, the bureau's activities fell into two broad categories: the control or eradication of animals harmful to agricultural productivity, and the conservation and protection of wildlife species endangered by humans.

Animal Damage Control

Throughout the late 1800s, farmers had increasingly complained about the damaging impact of predators and rodents on agricultural crops and livestock. The states, many of which had enacted antipredator laws, began to look to the Division of Biological Survey for help in reducing predator and rodent populations. The division, and later the Bureau of Biological Survey, responded

A hungry coyote closes in on his prey. Pressure by farmers to protect their livestock and crops from predators and pests led to the passage of animal-damage-control legislation in 1931.

between 1888 and 1914 by conducting a number of studies and demonstrations of animal-damage-control techniques, such as trapping and poisoning. By 1914, however, it became clear that even with the bureau's assistance, the states were fighting a losing battle against predators and rodents. This fact—and constant lobbying by the western states, where animal damage was most serious—led Congress to appropriate a small amount of money to the bureau for testing predator-control techniques. This first direct congressional appropriation for animal damage control marked a turning point in the federal government's involvement with the issue. The following year, Congress increased its commitment by appropriating $125,000 for a bureau program in Texas to kill wolves and coyotes, which were attacking local livestock. The bureau's animal-damage-control efforts were a success: In 1919, the bureau estimated that its rodent-control activities had resulted in a savings of $14 million in food nationwide.

The animal-damage-control program became large enough by 1929 to warrant its own division within the bureau—the Division of Predator and Rodent Control. Despite the success and growth of this program, western farmers continued to press Congress for additional federal assistance in combating predators. Their lobbying resulted in the 1931 passage of the Animal

Damage Control Act. This legislation expanded the scope of the bureau's animal-damage-control activities, which had previously been limited to federally owned lands, to include state, territorial, and private lands. The 1931 act established the first clear-cut statutory authority for federal efforts in this area, authorizing the bureau to conduct research on controlling or eradicating specific predators, including wolves and mountain lions, as well as other animals that were harmful to crops, livestock, wild game, fur-bearing animals, and birds.

Protecting Wildlife

Although the bureau was destroying or controlling harmful species, it was also seeking to protect certain species whose existence was threatened by human activity. Throughout the late 19th century, many species of wildlife were relentlessly hunted until their numbers fell to a dangerously low level. Some, including the buffalo, were on the verge of extinction. Although hunting for sport and study (for example, collecting museum specimens) was quite common, hunting for profit—called market hunting—took the heaviest toll on wildlife. The states attempted to curb market hunting by passing laws restricting or prohibiting the export of game killed within a state's borders. By 1899, half of the states had such laws. Many states went even further, establishing closed seasons during which it was illegal to kill game for any reason. But despite these efforts, the states had only limited success in halting market hunting.

Adding to the public's uneasy relationship with wildlife was the problem of unrestricted importation of non-native animal species. Although many imports, such as beef cattle, proved beneficial to humans, other imports created havoc in their new homeland. One of the best examples of this problem is the English sparrow, which was introduced into the United States, via New York, in 1851. Once settled in Boston, Massachusetts, the sparrow reproduced at an astonishing rate and became a public nuisance: It displaced many native bird species, dirtied the city with its droppings, and created a noise problem. Concerned citizens petitioned the mayor to do something about the sparrows, and the mayor responded by sending out a force of men to destroy the pest's nesting sites and eggs. Within 3 weeks 1,000 eggs and 4,000 nests were destroyed. The sparrow population would have been further decimated were it not for complaints from those who felt that this systematic extermination was unwarranted and inhumane.

The states' inability to curb market hunting and the general concern over the unrestricted importation of birds and animals into the country led to the passage of the Lacey Act on May 25, 1900. Administered by the Bureau of Biological Survey, the act had two goals: the suppression of market hunting through federal enforcement of state wildlife-conservation laws, and restriction of importation of birds and animals harmful to agricultural and other human interests. The act's first goal was accomplished by making it illegal to transport any bird or animal across state lines if it had been killed in violation of state laws—a provision that virtually eliminated market hunting. To enforce this provision, the act required all interstate shipments containing dead animals or birds, or parts thereof, to be accompanied by the name and address of the shipper as well as a description of the shipment's contents. Thus, inspectors stationed at freight and express offices throughout the country could quickly identify parcels for further investigation and, if necessary, initiate legal action against shippers who were found to have broken the law. The act's second goal was met by prohibiting the importation into the United States of any wild bird or animal without a permit from the Department of Agriculture. The Lacey Act also explicitly forbade the importation of certain notoriously harmful species, including the mongoose and the English sparrow, except when they were to be placed in scientific or museum collections. Finally, the act authorized the secretary of agriculture to adopt measures deemed necessary for the preservation and restoration of wild birds and those hunted for sport (called game birds).

The Lacey Act has been amended many times. The most significant amendment, added in 1935, extended the act's prohibition on transportation across state lines to cover birds and animals killed in violation of U.S. law or the laws of any other country. The Lacey Act also served as the model for another important federal wildlife law. As written, the Lacey Act applied only to "wild animals or birds"—coverage that was interpreted as excluding fish. Yet certain species of fish are also endangered by human activities. To remedy this apparent oversight, in 1926 Congress passed the Black Bass Act, providing to two species of fish commonly referred to as black bass the same protection that the Lacey Act gave to birds and animals. Although the Lacey Act was placed under the jurisdiction of the Biological Survey, the Black Bass Act was administered by the Bureau of Fisheries.

Foreign and Migratory Birds

Fish were not the only sort of wildlife that Congress felt needed protection beyond that afforded by the Lacey Act. By 1913, a growing number of people, including nature lovers and biologists, began expressing concern over the fate of two groups of birds: those killed on foreign soil and then imported into the United States to satisfy fashion trends, and those that migrated great distances over the North American continent. These concerns were addressed by Congress in 1913 with the passage of the Federal Tariff Act and the Migratory Bird Act. The Federal Tariff Act forbade the importation into the United States of any feathers or bird parts except those used for scientific purposes. The Migratory Bird Act was more ambitious in scope. It placed all migratory birds passing through the United States under the custody and protection of the federal government. This meant that the hunting of such birds was prohibited unless approved by the Bureau of Biological Survey. The act also prohibited the hunting of migratory birds during their breeding periods in the spring and limited the hunting season to three and one-half months.

The Migratory Bird Act was promptly challenged by the states as an infringement of their constitutional right, guaranteed by the 10th Amendment, to manage wildlife within state borders. The court that heard the case ruled in favor of the states' claim, finding the act to be unconstitutional. While the case was on appeal to the Supreme Court, the Senate passed legislation that gave the president the authority to negotiate a treaty with Great Britain, which was

A flock of snow geese in their winter habitat in New Mexico. The Migratory Bird Treaty Act of 1918 authorized the Bureau of Biological Survey to regulate the hunting seasons on such birds, which are dependent on safe passage between breeding grounds in the North and wintering habitat in the South.

President Woodrow Wilson was able to circumvent the states' objections to federal regulation of migratory bird hunting by using his international treaty-making powers. Wilson negotiated a treaty with Great Britain that protected migratory birds through a range of hunting regulations.

acting on behalf of Canada, for the protection of migratory birds. Because the constitutionality of the federal government's treaty-making powers was not likely to be contested, this migratory bird treaty was able to achieve what the Migratory Bird Act was intended to accomplish without being challenged by the states. President Woodrow Wilson's use of this treaty-making authority resulted in the Convention for the Protection of Migratory Birds, which was signed by the United States and Great Britain on August 16, 1916, and ratified by the Senate shortly thereafter. As a result of the president's action, the appeal to the Supreme Court was dropped.

Among its provisions, the Convention for the Protection of Migratory Birds set open and closed hunting seasons for migratory game birds, prohibited the hunting of insectivorous birds (those that feed on insects), and established a 10-year moratorium on the killing of certain species of game birds. Two years after the ratification of the convention, Congress passed the Migratory Bird Treaty Act of 1918, which provided statutory authority to carry out the terms of the convention within the United States. The Treaty Act thus gave the Bureau of Biological Survey the responsibility for regulating the hunting of birds protected by the convention. In line with this responsibility, the bureau enacted regulations that limited the number of birds that could be taken by hunters and prohibited the killing of certain migratory, nongame birds that were in need of special protection.

The states were not happy with the Migratory Bird Treaty Act for the same reasons they had objected to the Migratory Bird Act five years earlier. Again, the states claimed that they owned the wildlife within their borders and could manage it as they saw fit. This time, however, the case did make it to the Supreme Court. In 1920, the court ruled in favor of the federal government, upholding the government's treaty-making power as a source of authority to regulate migratory birds. Based on this precedent, the federal government later signed similar migratory bird treaties with Mexico (1930), Japan (1972), and the Soviet Union (1976).

At the time the Supreme Court was considering the constitutionality of the Migratory Bird Treaty Act, it appeared as if the populations of migratory birds were holding their own. But soon afterward, the situation worsened. The draining and plowing of wetlands—ponds, swamps, bogs, and marshes—that had begun during World War I in an effort to provide more farmland to produce more food continued well into the 1920s and destroyed many of the breeding grounds used by migratory birds. In addition, the increased mobility of the public, made possible by the mass production of automobiles, enabled hunters to travel farther, faster, and more frequently in search of migratory game birds. With the limited enforcement of federal and state migratory bird protection laws, populations of such birds declined in the 1920s.

To stem the decline in migratory bird populations, Congress created a mechanism to preserve the wetland habitat upon which such birds depend. The Migratory Bird Conservation Act of 1929 authorized the federal government to acquire migratory bird refuges through purchase, donation, or rental agreement and prohibited migratory bird hunting on the refuges year-round. The timing of this act could not have been worse. With the onset of the Great Depression in 1929, money became extremely scarce. And because the protection of migratory birds was hardly a national priority, Congress appropriated minimal funds for the acquisition of refuges. Not only did financial resources dry up, but the wetlands did, too: During the early 1930s, a severe drought hit the midwestern United States, creating a condition known as a dust bowl.

The lack of federal funding for refuge development, coupled with disastrous climatic conditions, resulted in a further reduction in migratory bird populations.

A plowed field encroaches on wetland habitat. The draining and plowing of wetland areas in the early 20th century reduced the amount of natural habitat available to support migratory bird populations.

Conservationists searched for alternative ways to fund the acquisition of refuge lands. Under the leadership of Jay "Ding" Darling, a political cartoonist and later head of the Biological Survey, a group of conservationists devised a funding mechanism that was ultimately included in the Migratory Bird Hunting and Conservation Stamp Act, passed on March 16, 1934. Under this act—commonly referred to as the Duck Stamp Act—every hunter 16 years of age or older was required to purchase a one-dollar Federal Migratory Bird Hunting and Conservation Stamp. The proceeds from these sales were placed in a Migratory Bird Conservation Account, which was used for research and the development, purchase, and maintenance of migratory bird sanctuaries and other wildlife refuges visited by migratory game birds. Over the years, funds from the Duck Stamp Act have made possible the acquisition of numerous sanctuaries and refuges. As land prices increased over time, so did the cost of the duck stamp: By 1988, the stamp cost $10.

J. "Ding" Darling, a political cartoonist for the Des Moines, Iowa, Register, *at work on one of his well-known wildlife drawings. Darling devised the duck stamp to fund the acquisition of waterfowl refuges in the 1930s and designed the first stamp himself.*

Wildlife Refuges

The creation of refuges to protect wildlife was popular long before the passage of either the Migratory Bird Conservation Act or the Duck Stamp Act. Indeed, the roots of the refuge idea go all the way back to 1870, when California established the first government-owned wildlife refuge in what is now known as Lake Merrit in downtown Oakland. But it was not until Theodore Roosevelt's presidency (1901–9) that the development of refuges became a federal concern.

Considered by many to be the nation's most conservation-minded president, Roosevelt had developed a keen appreciation of nature and the need for

Although he was an avid hunter, Theodore Roosevelt believed in the wise conservation and management of wildlife resources. Roosevelt established the nation's first 53 wildlife refuges during his 8 years in office.

Brown pelicans in their natural habitat on Florida's Pelican Island National Wildlife Refuge. President Theodore Roosevelt set aside the five-acre federally owned nesting area as the nation's first wildlife refuge in 1903.

natural-resource protection through his hiking and hunting trips into the wilderness. Once in office, he instituted landmark conservation measures. Roosevelt's interest was piqued in 1903 when his friend Frank Chapman, an ornithologist, asked him to sell a federally owned pelican breeding area off the Florida coast so that it could become a bird sanctuary. Because a law prohibited the sale of federal property, Roosevelt found another means of accomplishing similar ends. On March 14, 1903, the president issued an executive order establishing the breeding area, called Pelican Island, as the first federal refuge. By the time Roosevelt left office in 1909 he had created 53 refuges on federal property.

Congress followed Roosevelt's example in 1905 when it created the Wichita Mountains Wildlife Refuge in Oklahoma. In 1908, the American Bison Society challenged the federal government to establish a refuge by offering the nation 50 buffalo if adequate provisions could be made for their care. Congress responded by authorizing the president to use federal funds to purchase land for the protection of wildlife. In 1909, President William Taft took advantage of this new authority by purchasing 12,800 acres of the Flathead Indian Reservation in Montana, creating what is now called the National Bison Range. In October of that year, 37 buffalo were introduced onto the range. By the late 1980s, the descendants of those 37 buffalo numbered nearly 400.

The remaining years of the bureau's existence witnessed the continued growth of refuges. At the end of 1914, the bureau was responsible for 65 refuges, all but 5 of which were for birds (the 5 were established for big game). By 1928, there were 80 refuges managed by the Biological Survey, spread out over more than half the states in the nation. And by 1940, with the help of the Migratory Bird Conservation Act of 1929 and the Duck Stamp Act, the bureau controlled more than 250 refuges totaling more than 13 million acres.

The last major changes in the bureau's responsibilities resulted from the passage of the Fish and Wildlife Coordination Act of 1934 and the Federal Aid in Wildlife Restoration Act, passed in 1937. Together, these acts significantly bolstered the abilities of the federal government and the states to preserve wildlife. Among its provisions affecting wildlife, the Fish and Wildlife Coordination Act authorized the bureau to use the waters of any federally built or licensed dam as a nesting or resting area for migratory birds, to develop a national conservation program, and to assist federal and state agencies in fighting wildlife diseases and enhancing game populations. It also authorized the bureau to study how pollution affects wildlife and to conduct surveys of wildlife species inhabiting public lands in order to better manage them.

The Federal Aid in Wildlife Restoration Act, better known as the Pittman-Robertson Act, was based on Congress's conclusion that improvement in the effectiveness of wildlife management nationwide was dependent upon the federal government giving the states more assistance. The reasoning behind this conclusion is clear: Then, as now, the majority of wildlife was on nonfederal land, over which the states retained primary control. Although strong federal wildlife management was important, strong state programs were essential.

The Pittman-Robertson Act sought to strengthen the states' ability to manage wildlife by offering them financial assistance to be used in developing wildlife-management programs. The act established a federal fund to aid wildlife restoration, the money for which came from a federal excise tax on firearms and ammunition. The states became eligible to receive the funds by submitting proposals for wildlife projects—such as conducting population surveys, purchasing wildlife habitat, and stocking wildlife—to the bureau. If the project was approved, the wildlife restoration fund would supply up to 75 percent of the project's cost, allocated to the state fish and game departments according to a formula based on the state's size and the number of hunting licenses it has issued. (The state would provide the remaining 25 percent or more of the project's cost.) Between 1938 and 1966, about $30 million was granted to the states under Pittman-Robertson; lands purchased with these funds totaled 2.8 million acres.

As with its fisheries-resources programs, the federal government could, by 1940, look back on a number of accomplishments in the area of wildlife protection and management. A large national wildlife refuge system had been established, market hunting was no longer a threat to animal populations, harmful predators and rodents were being brought under control, and the Supreme Court had made it clear that the federal government had considerable authority to regulate wildlife, specifically migratory birds, within the nation's borders.

The Creation of the Fish and Wildlife Service

During the 1930s, the United States suffered a widespread economic depression in which millions of Americans lost their jobs. According to President Franklin D. Roosevelt, one of the many causes of the depression had to do with poor natural-resource management. One of the steps Roosevelt took to improve this situation was to increase the coordination of government agencies involved in natural-resource work. The rapid expansion of many of these agencies during the 1930s had caused the duplication of efforts and, in some cases, direct competition. Roosevelt felt that by increasing coordination among the agencies the government could achieve greater efficiency. To this end, he signed Reorganization Plan II on July 1, 1939, which transferred the Bureau of Fisheries and the Bureau of Biological Survey into the Department of the Interior. One year later, on June 30, 1940, Reorganization Plan III merged the two bureaus, creating the Fish and Wildlife Service (FWS). With the creation of the service, the nation's fish and wildlife activities entered a new period of growth.

Fish ladders enable anadromous fish to travel from the ocean, where they spend most of their lives, to their upstream spawning grounds. In the mid-20th century, the Fish and Wildlife Service gained added authority to ensure that dams planned for construction include these devices.

THREE

Renewed Protective Legislation

Soon after the Fish and Wildlife Service was created in 1940, the service's role in protecting, enhancing, and conserving the nation's fish and wildlife grew considerably. In 1946, Congress reevaluated the Fish and Wildlife Coordination Act of 1934 and, after finding its powers to be too limited, amended the act to expand the FWS's authority concerning federal projects that posed a potential risk to fish and wildlife. The original act required federal agencies to consult with the Bureau of Fisheries before constructing or licensing the construction of a dam to give the bureau an opportunity to recommend the installation of fish ladders. The 1946 amendment extended this power to require consultation with FWS and the appropriate state agencies not only prior to dam construction but whenever any body of water was going to be diverted, impounded, or otherwise controlled as a result of a federally sponsored project. (Examples of such projects include canal construction, deepening a river channel, or any other modification of a stream or body of water.) In addition, the goal of this consultation was expanded from aiding fish migration to encompass the protection of all wildlife resources.

Managing the Nation's Fisheries

During the mid-1940s, at the same time that Congress amended the Fish and Wildlife Coordination Act, millions of veterans were returning home from World War II. One result of peacetime, in addition to the economic strength of a country grown strong through war-related industry, was an increased amount of leisure time for the average American. During the next few years a large number of those Americans chose to spend their free time fishing. The increase in fishing, however, caused a decrease in the populations of certain prized species. This trend alarmed both conservationists and sportsmen, who argued that without federal assistance the states would be unable to keep recreational fisheries from being depleted.

In 1950, Congress took steps to help the states manage their recreational fisheries by passing the Federal Aid in Fish Restoration Act, commonly referred to as the Dingell-Johnson Act. The Dingell-Johnson Act did for fish

Workers stock a lake with fish in the mid-1930s. In 1950, the passage of the Dingell-Johnson Act made funds available to support such state projects designed to enhance sport and recreational fisheries.

Massachusetts fishermen pull up a haul of fish in 1942. The passage of the Dingell-Johnson Act, which provided funding for sport and recreational fishing projects, led commercial fishermen to call for the creation of an agency to safeguard their interests.

what the Pittman-Robertson Act had done for wildlife. Like the Pittman-Robertson Act, which received its funding from a tax on firearms and ammunition, the funds for Dingell-Johnson came from a federal excise tax on fishing equipment such as rods and reels. Each state was required to submit proposals to the FWS for projects to restore or manage marine or freshwater fish used for sport or recreational fishing. Projects could include restocking depleted fisheries, gathering facts needed to establish regulatory controls over fish populations, or creating fishery-resources education programs. Once a project was approved, the state became eligible for federal funds that could pay as much as 75 percent of the project's cost. These funds were distributed to the state according to its size and the number of fishing licenses held by its citizens. The state itself was responsible for providing the remaining 25 percent or more of the project's cost.

The Fish and Wildlife Act of 1956

The passage of the Dingell-Johnson Act greatly disturbed commercial fishermen, who felt that the FWS was paying too much attention to recreational and sport fishing at the expense of commercial fishing. Commercial fishing interests began lobbying Congress for the creation of a separate government agency that would be more attentive to their concerns. In 1956, Congress considered a bill that would remove all fishing regulation from the FWS and assign it to a new agency. This move was strongly opposed by conservation groups, who wanted the FWS to retain authority over fisheries activities because of the service's emphasis on conservation. Congress attempted to appease both sides by passing the Fish and Wildlife Act of 1956, which established within the Department of the Interior the United States Fish and Wildlife Service (USFWS), consisting of two bureaus: the Bureau of Sport Fisheries and Wildlife and the Bureau of Commercial Fisheries.

The responsibilities of the Bureau of Sport Fisheries and Wildlife and the Bureau of Commercial Fisheries were similar to those held by the former bureaus of Biological Survey and Fisheries, respectively. For example, the Bureau of Sport Fisheries and Wildlife was given responsibility for managing wildlife refuges, and the Bureau of Commercial Fisheries was required to collect statistics on commercial fisheries. In addition to establishing the USFWS and its two bureaus, the Fish and Wildlife Act expanded the service's authority for acquiring refuges, established a national policy of maintaining and increasing public recreational use of fish and wildlife resources, and encouraged the development of a strong commercial fishing industry.

Expanding the Fish and Wildlife Coordination Act

In 1958, Congress once again amended the Fish and Wildlife Coordination Act of 1934, claiming that the 1946 amendment had not achieved satisfactory results. The new amendment created a more effective integration of fish and wildlife conservation programs and water-resource-development projects, requiring that fish and wildlife conservation be given equal consideration with other concerns in the planning of federally sponsored or licensed projects. As in the original act, the 1958 amendment provided for a consultation process between the USFWS, state wildlife agencies, and the sponsoring federal agency to decide whether a project would harm fish and wildlife. Reports submitted to Congress for authorization of a project were required to include estimates of the project's impact on fish and wildlife. They were also to describe the projected benefits of any changes in construction recommended by the secretary of the interior. If the project was found to pose a risk to fish and wildlife, the secretary of the interior could recommend that the agency not proceed with construction or licensing. It was then up to the sponsoring agency to decide if it would comply with this recommendation.

One case in which a federal agency decided to take the service's advice involved Marco Island, located on the Gulf Coast of Florida. In 1964, the Deltona Corporation bought 10,000 acres of Florida coastal lands including Marco Island with the intention of building a five-site residential community. Deltona was required to obtain a permit for each of the five stages of construction from the U.S. Army Corps of Engineers, the federal agency with jurisdiction over construction activities in the navigable waters of the United States. The corps granted permits for the first two stages of construction in 1964 and 1969. However, when Deltona applied for the last three permits that it needed to complete the project, it ran into trouble. These permits would have allowed the company to fill in a wetland area for one of its housing sites. Based on great public

Real estate developments such as this one in southern Florida often involved filling in wetland areas on which many species of fish and wildlife depend. The 1958 amendment to the Fish and Wildlife Coordination Act of 1934 required that such projects be monitored by the USFWS to safeguard wildlife interests.

opposition to the project and a USFWS recommendation—following the consultation process required under the Fish and Wildlife Coordination Act, during which the service argued that the wetlands were too valuable to be destroyed—the corps refused to grant two of the permits. This decision is noteworthy because in denying the permits the corps decided that protecting the wetlands—and the fish and wildlife they supported—was more important than the economic benefits, such as jobs and sales, that would have come with the completion of the project.

The Fish and Wildlife Coordination Act of 1934, as amended, was the first statute requiring federal agencies to consider fish and wildlife values in planning their activities. Similar protective legislation soon followed the act and its amendments. The Sikes Act, passed in 1960, grew out of Congress's desire to conserve and protect fish and wildlife resources located on the nation's vast military bases. The act authorized the USFWS to work with the Department of Defense and the appropriate state agencies to develop fish and wildlife management plans for the lands under the department's control. Today, these plans cover nearly 19 million of the more than 24 million acres of Defense Department land. In 1974, the Sikes Act was amended to require that fish and wildlife management plans also be drawn up for lands under the jurisdiction of the departments of agriculture and energy. At a minimum, such plans were required to provide for habitat modifications or improvements and offer protection to threatened and endangered species.

Creating a National Wildlife Refuge System

The lands under the control of the Department of Defense were not the only ones to receive congressional attention in the 1960s. Ever since President Theodore Roosevelt created the first federal wildlife refuge on Pelican Island in 1903, the refuge system had grown considerably. This growth was somewhat disjointed, however, because through the early 1960s there was no single law that spelled out how refuges were to be managed. The National Wildlife Refuge System Administration Act of 1966 changed all that; it established the National Wildlife Refuge System and brought all wildlife refuges, along with many other protected areas, such as game ranges, under control of the USFWS. The act's most important provision authorized the service to allow any area within the National Wildlife Refuge System to be used for any purpose as long as it had determined that such use was compatible with the purposes for which the area was established. For example, hiking could be

A refuge officer steers visitors through the twisted waterways of Georgia's Okefenokee National Wildlife Refuge in the late 1950s. The compatible-use concept that allows such activity within refuges has been a topic of perpetual disagreement; in 1971, outboard motors such as this one were prohibited from use in Okefenokee.

allowed in a refuge established to protect migratory birds as long as the hiking did not harm the birds themselves. The compatible-use concept has since sparked many controversies. One of the most common disputes is the debate between hunters and conservationists in which the latter contend that hunting is incompatible with the purposes for which refuges are established. Resolving such controversies over compatible use continues to be a difficult problem.

Reform in Animal-Damage-Control Programs

In the early 1960s, there was a sudden, increased public awareness of the effects on the environment and on wildlife of industrial pollutants and modern, man-made toxins. In 1962, *Silent Spring*, a controversial new book by former Fish and Wildlife Service biologist Rachel Carson, shocked the public with its description of the dangers to the natural environment of chemical pesticides (poisons that are used to control insects). At the same time, the dangerous buildup of other environmental pollutants such as automobile exhaust and industrial refuse captured public attention. One result of this awareness was a new interest in evaluating the federal government's animal-damage-control program, which had been subject to little public scrutiny since the passage of the Animal Damage Control Act of 1931.

Many people, including conservationists and those concerned with the humane treatment of animals, believed that the use of poisons was causing an excessive number of deaths among nontarget animals—those not intended to be killed. For example, until the early 1960s fish and wildlife agencies routinely used whole animal carcasses laced with Compound 1080, a highly lethal poison, to kill coyotes. Although this method of predator control was quite effective, the poison-laced carcasses also attracted and killed other animals, such as bears and eagles. Critics of these methods also believed that an excessive amount of poison was being used.

In 1963, Secretary of the Interior Stewart Udall—a dedicated conservationist—established an advisory board to investigate the USFWS's control efforts

This sheep is fitted with a collar containing the highly toxic Compound 1080, a poison that will kill any animal that feeds on the sheep. The USFWS's predator-control program came under attack in the 1960s from environmentalists and animal-rights advocates who claimed that such methods also killed nontarget animals and distributed an excessive amount of poison into the environment.

Secretary of the Interior Stewart L. Udall—a staunch conservationist— paddles down a Missouri river during a 1961 inspection of an area proposed for national park status.

and to decide if the concerns about the agency were well founded. The resulting Leopold Report, named after Starker Leopold, an eminent zoologist who was the board's chairman, determined that the amount of animal damage control conducted nationwide was far in excess of that required to combat predator and rodent damage. The report also claimed that the distribution of highly lethal poisons often violated USFWS regulations. To rectify these problems, the report recommended a wide range of measures, including additional research on the development of species-specific control methods that would spare nontarget animals and tightening controls over the distribution and use of poisons.

Although the Leopold Report prompted changes in animal-damage-control strategies, many of its recommendations met with opposition. As a result, an advisory board was convened in 1971 to further investigate the animal-damage-control program. The board's report basically reiterated the findings of the Leopold Report; it also recommended banning all poisons. The following year, President Richard Nixon signed an executive order making it illegal to use poisons for predator control on federal lands or in federal programs. (This order, however, was repealed by President Ronald Reagan shortly after he took office in 1981; thus, poisons were still being used by the federal government for animal damage control throughout the 1980s. Most of the USFWS's traditional predator-control activities were transferred to the U.S. Department of Agriculture during the same period.)

Reorganization of the USFWS

The year 1970 saw another milestone in the evolution of the USFWS: President Nixon signed a reorganization plan that transferred the Bureau of Commercial Fisheries to the newly created National Marine Fisheries Service (NMFS), an agency within the Department of Commerce. The transfer gave the NMFS most of the marine-related duties formerly held by the bureau, while the responsibility for inland fisheries management remained with the Bureau of Sport Fisheries and Wildlife. Then, on April 22, 1974, the Bureau of Sport Fisheries and Wildlife was redesignated the United States Fish and Wildlife Service. Foremost among the responsibilities of the reorganized USFWS was the implementation of three laws: the Marine Mammal Protection Act of 1972, the Endangered Species Act of 1973, and the Fish and Wildlife Conservation Act, passed in 1980.

The Marine Mammal Protection Act

Public concern over the fate of marine mammals first surfaced in the last half of the 19th century, when the success of the whaling industry resulted in a sharp decline in the populations of commercially valuable whale species, including sperm and right whales. During the 20th century this concern spread to other marine mammals, such as fur seals, manatees, and sea otters, whose populations were also being decimated by human activities, primarily hunting. Although public sentiment resulted in federal actions to protect certain marine mammals, especially whales, by the late 1960s many groups felt that more comprehensive steps were needed to protect the animals from disappearing altogether. Scientists argued that these mammals needed stronger protection because of the important role they played in the marine environment. The whaling industry wanted stricter management of marine mammals in order to avoid overharvesting that could ultimately destroy its livelihood. And some citizens, labeled "protectionists," pushed for a ban on the taking of all marine mammals.

Responding to these diverse interests, Congress passed the Marine Mammal Protection Act of 1972 (MMPA). The main feature of the act is a

The success of the New England whaling industry caused the whale population to fall to a dangerously low level by the late 19th century. In 1972, the Marine Mammal Protection Act charged the Interior Department and the Department of Commerce with protecting whales and other marine mammals threatened by hunting and other human activities.

moratorium, of unspecified duration, on the taking of marine mammals by any person under the jurisdiction of United States law, including foreign boats fishing within 200 miles of the U.S. coastline. *Taking* is defined broadly to include killing, hunting, capturing, or harassing. The act also banned the importation or sale of marine mammals or products made from them. There are a number of exceptions to these rules. For example, marine mammals can be collected for scientific reasons or for public display in aquariums and zoos. In addition, certain native peoples of the Alaskan region are allowed to hunt marine mammals for food and to use marine mammal parts to make clothing and traditional handicrafts such as bone carvings.

The responsibility for enforcing the MMPA is divided between the Department of Commerce and the Department of the Interior; within these departments, responsibility is delegated to the NMFS and the USFWS, respectively. The NMFS is responsible for whales, dolphins, seals, and sea lions; the USFWS has responsibility for dugongs, manatees, polar bears, sea otters, and

The manatee is one of the marine mammals protected by the USFWS under the Marine Mammal Protection Act. The service also guards other land-oriented marine mammals such as dugongs, polar bears, sea otters, and walruses.

walruses. The split in responsibility between the NMFS and the USFWS is a result of the 1970 transfer of the Bureau of Commercial Fisheries to the Department of Commerce. Supervision of those marine mammals considered more land-oriented remained with the Bureau of Sport Fisheries and Wildlife in the Department of the Interior; jurisdiction over the other animals went to the Department of Commerce.

In carrying out the provisions of the MMPA, both the NMFS and the USFWS must consult with the Marine Mammal Commission, an independent advisory group created by the act, and must keep the commission up to date on their activities. The commission's responsibilities include reviewing the status of marine mammals, monitoring U.S. activities relating to marine mammals, and making recommendations on ways to improve marine mammal management strategies. A group of scientific experts aids the commission in carrying out these duties.

The Endangered Species Act

One year after the Marine Mammal Protection Act became law, Congress strengthened the federal government's ability to protect imperiled wildlife by passing the Endangered Species Act of 1973. This was not the first time legislative action was taken specifically on the issue of endangered species; seven years earlier Congress had passed the Endangered Species Preservation Act of 1966, which directed the service to keep a listing of endangered species and to acquire refuges for these animals. However, the 1966 act did not provide for enforcement procedures to protect the listed species. Three years later, Congress passed the Endangered Species Conservation Act of 1969. This act made it illegal to import, export, or take any listed species. Although the two acts afforded protection to endangered species, by the early 1970s conservationists, legislators, and the public felt that a more comprehensive and effective program was needed to prevent the extinction of these animals. Congress passed the 1973 act to create that program.

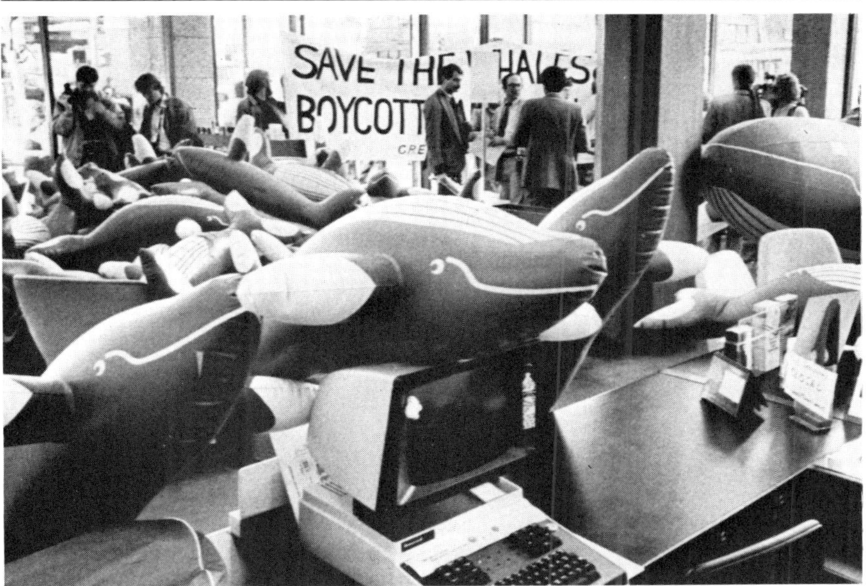

Members of Greenpeace, an environmentalist organization, occupy the San Francisco offices of Japan Air Lines in 1985 to protest Japan's whaling practices. During the 1970s, animal-rights organizations such as Greenpeace contributed to the passage of the Marine Mammal Protection Act and the Endangered Species Act.

The Endangered Species Act is a complex and extensive piece of legislation the primary goal of which is to protect and conserve two groups of animal and plant species: *endangered species*, or those "in danger of extinction throughout all or a significant portion of [their] range" (a range is a species' entire existing population); and *threatened species*, animals not currently in danger of becoming extinct but "likely to become an endangered species within the foreseeable future throughout all or a significant portion of [their] range." The act's coverage includes animals in the United States as well as foreign species. In addition to protecting the animals and plants themselves, the act also protects the habitat upon which they depend. This habitat, labeled the *critical habitat* by the act, consists of those areas that are essential to the continued survival of the species.

Supporters of the Endangered Species Act presented many reasons why such species should be protected by law. Some felt that because of the intricate connections between living organisms, the destruction or removal of a particular species could have unforeseen and quite damaging consequences to humans. They cited as an example of such a situation a species of hippopotamus that was removed from certain rivers in East Africa because it was eating valuable food crops along the shore. Although this action protected the crops on shore, it drastically reduced another food source upon which the local people depended, a subspecies of fish called *tilapia*. It was discovered that hippopotamus feces fertilized the algae growing in the river that, in turn, was eaten by the tilapia. Thus, after the hippopotamus was removed, tilapia populations dwindled, and one food-loss problem was simply substituted for another.

Other supporters of the Endangered Species Act argued that endangered or threatened species deserve protection because of the role they may play in solving human health problems. One estimate claims that nearly 25 percent of the prescription drugs dispensed annually in the United States contain substances derived from plants or animals. Some very rare species of evening primrose have recently been found to produce a chemical that may aid in the treatment of arthritis and hardening of the arteries. In addition to providing substances that can be used to cure disease, specific animal species are invaluable in disease and drug research and testing. For example, mollusks (snails, clams, and other animals with a soft, unsegmented body and an external or internal shell) are resistant to cancer; scientists are now studying these animals in the hope of learning how to prevent the occurrence of this disease among humans.

Finally, there were those supporters of the Endangered Species Act who viewed all species of wildlife and plants as having a basic right to life.

A USFWS agent displays a confiscated alligator hide. Under the Endangered Species Act, it is illegal to import, export, sell, or possess an endangered species, such as the alligator, or products made from the body of an endangered species.

Therefore, just as it is illegal for one human to kill another, these people argued, it should be against the law for humans, through their actions, to cause the extinction of any of the species with which they share the planet.

The first and most important step in carrying out the provisions of the Endangered Species Act is listing those species that are either endangered or threatened. The authority to list a species is divided between the USFWS and the NMFS. With a few exceptions, the USFWS has authority over the listing of freshwater and terrestrial (land-dwelling) species, whereas the NMFS controls the listing of marine species. The listing process can be initiated either by the agency or through a petition from any interested citizen, but it is up to the agency to decide if it will actually propose a species for listing. The agency must advertise the proposed listing in the *Federal Register* (the official government publication that gives notice of executive orders, federal agencies' policies and proposals, and the like) and request comments on it. After the

An Eskimo girl on Alaska's Nunivak Island. A special provision of the Endangered Species Act allows Alaskan natives to use endangered species for food and to make handicrafts and clothing, such as the fur bonnet worn by this girl.

comments are reviewed, the agency makes the final decision as to whether or not the species will be listed.

Once a species is listed it becomes subject to the act's protection, which varies depending on the species' status. Endangered species cannot be taken anywhere in the United States, its territorial waters, or on the open ocean by anybody who is under U.S. jurisdiction. Just as with the MMPA, the definition of *taking* in the Endangered Species Act is quite broad and includes harassing, harming, hunting, trapping, or collecting. The act also prohibits the importation, exportation, sale, or possession of any endangered species taken in violation of the act.

The level of protection given to threatened species can be quite different than that given to endangered species. According to the act, the agency has the discretion to devise whatever regulations it deems necessary in order to conserve threatened species. Thus, the agency may apply the same prohibitions to endangered and threatened species, or it may decide that threatened species require less protection than those on the endangered list. The penalties for violating the act's prohibitions and regulations are severe, and, depending on the violation, can result in one year of imprisonment and up to $20,000 in fines. There are instances, however, in which taking can be allowed under permit. For example, the act resembles the MMPA by allowing certain Alaskan natives to hunt listed species for food and to use the inedible parts in making handicrafts and clothing. The taking of listed species may also be allowed for scientific purposes.

The ultimate goal of the Endangered Species Act is not simply to list species, but to get them off the list so that they no longer require the act's protection. To do this, the agency in charge of managing the species in question prepares a recovery plan detailing the actions that should be taken to restore the species' population. Because it is difficult to measure the success of such recovery plans, the USFWS and the NMFS often cannot precisely determine whether the overall status of a species is improving, getting worse, or staying the same. Nevertheless, there are examples of both successes and failures in the endangered species program.

The population of the Aleutian Canada goose, once an abundant migratory bird, was reduced to 800 by the mid-1970s as a result of predator introduction and hunting along the bird's migration routes and at its wintering areas. To stem the animal's precipitous decline, the USFWS listed it as an endangered species. This action, along with subsequent recovery efforts undertaken by the USFWS that included purchasing (and thus protecting by law) migration and wintering habitat and reducing predator populations, proved sufficient to

A flock of Aleutian Canada geese in the bird's Alaskan habitat. The USFWS successfully reversed the decline in the population of this species using the authority granted to it under the Endangered Species Act of 1973.

reverse the bird's decline. By the late 1980s, the Aleutian goose population had grown to more than 4,000, and the USFWS hoped to be able to take the goose off its endangered species list in the near future.

Unfortunately, the story of the California condor does not have such a happy ending. The condor, one of the rarest birds in the Western Hemisphere, is also one of the largest, weighing up to 22 pounds and having a wingspan of up to 10 feet. Efforts to protect the condor began as early as 1939 with the establishment of a 1,200-acre condor sanctuary in California. At that time between 40 and 70 condors were estimated to be in the wild. Fourteen years later, in 1953, the state of California passed a law to protect the birds. In 1967, the condor was placed on the first federal endangered species list. And in 1975, the first condor recovery plan was approved. Since that time a large number of groups, including the USFWS, the Forest Service, the California Department of Fish and Game, and the Interior Department's Bureau of Land Management have worked together to establish a captive breeding program for the condor and also to learn more about its behavior in the hope of finding ways to help it survive.

But by the late 1980s, despite these efforts, the condor population was at an all-time low. There were no condors left in the wild and only 28 in captivity. Those in captivity were kept at two breeding facilities: the Greater Los Angeles Zoo and the San Diego Wild Animal Park. The first condor to be hatched in captivity appeared in 1988, prompting optimism at the USFWS about the bird's future. The service had recently purchased a new wildlife refuge, Bitter Creek, located in California, to serve as home for condors released from the captive breeding program. The USFWS predicts that the breeding program will not begin producing the number of birds required to populate Bitter Creek National Wildlife Refuge until the early 1990s. The service is optimistic, but for now the California condor's fate hangs in the balance.

The fate of the California condor, an endangered species, remains uncertain. Despite USFWS efforts to revive the dwindling condor population, in the late 1980s the bird is thought to exist only in captivity.

One of the most important features of the Endangered Species Act is Section 7, which requires all federal agencies to ensure that actions they authorize, fund, or carry out do not jeopardize the continued existence of any endangered or threatened species. Section 7 also requires that such actions do not destroy or adversely modify the critical habitat of a listed species. Thus, before a federal agency proceeds with any action, such as building a dam, it must consult with either the USFWS or the NMFS to determine whether the proposed action threatens the existence of a listed species or its critical habitat. If during the consultation it is found that the action would place a listed species or its critical habitat in jeopardy, the action must be modified so that such danger is avoided. Although there have been thousands of Section 7 consultations, only a few hundred have identified a potential conflict between a project and the survival of a listed species, and only a handful of these have resulted in the delay or abandonment of a project. As hoped, since the passage of the Endangered Species Act federal agencies have increasingly considered their projects' impact on endangered species while the projects are still in the planning stages, thus minimizing both the potential risk to wildlife and the chances that such a risk will cause the delay or abandonment of a project.

One of the most publicized Section 7 controversies concerned a small, endangered species of fish called the snail darter. During the construction of

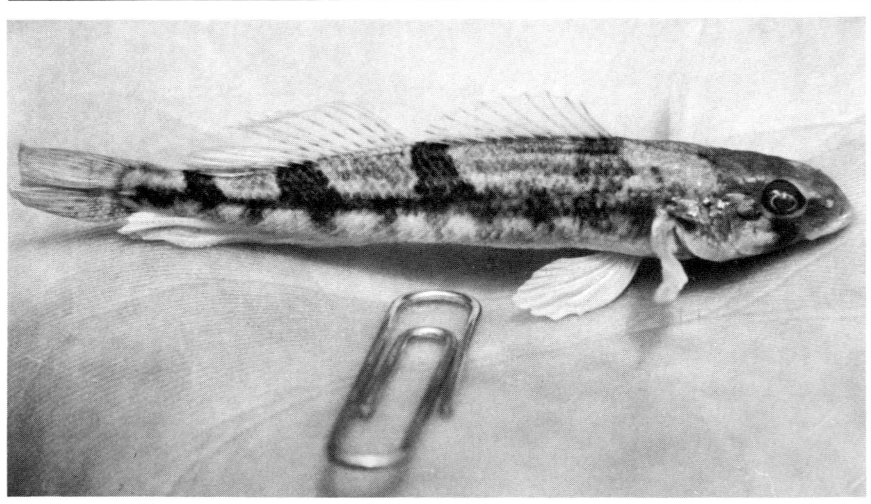

The tiny snail darter was the center of great controversy in the mid-1970s when environmentalists discovered that a dam under construction in Tennessee would destroy the fish's habitat.

the Tellico Dam in Tennessee in the mid-1970s, it was discovered that this federally sponsored project would most likely destroy the snail darter's entire known habitat. In 1976, using this information, environmental groups, including the Audubon Council of Tennessee, brought a legal suit against the government, charging that the dam's completion would jeopardize the continued existence of the endangered snail darter. The district court hearing the case agreed with these claims but refused to prevent the completion of the project for two reasons: First, the court noted that abandoning the project, which was far along in the construction process, would result in the loss of millions of dollars; second, the court argued that it was Congress's responsibility to balance the interests of development and wildlife protection, and that Congress had already made its decision by funding the project even after the endangerment of the snail darter had been discovered.

The district court's decision was reviewed by a court of appeals, which decided that the lower court had erred in its judgment. Specifically, the court of appeals held that because the completion of the dam would jeopardize the continued existence of an endangered species, the court had no other choice but to stop the project from going forward. In 1978, the Supreme Court reviewed this decision and upheld it in a six-to-three decision. In its ruling, the Supreme Court pointed out that the language of the Endangered Species Act plainly stated that any federally sponsored project that places a listed species or its critical habitat in jeopardy must be modified so that such jeopardy is avoided. Despite the Supreme Court's decision, the Tellico Dam was ultimately completed after Congress exempted the project from the Endangered Species Act in 1980. At the time, this congressional exemption was viewed by some as the first premeditated human decision to cause another species' extinction. As it turned out, however, the ultimate impact of the dam was not quite that drastic; although the snail darter population behind the dam was destroyed, additional populations of snail darters were soon found in other tributaries of the Tennessee River. Indeed, the discovery of these new populations was enough to downgrade the snail darter's status from endangered to threatened.

Another important provision of the Endangered Species Act is embodied in Section 6, which enables the states to become actively involved in the protection of endangered and threatened species. Once a state develops an endangered species program that meets certain federal requirements, it can enter into a cooperative agreement with either the USFWS or the NMFS, depending on the program's focus. The main incentive for entering into one of these agreements is financial; each state that does so becomes eligible for federal funding for its endangered species program.

Construction was delayed on Tennessee's Tellico Dam when environmentalists sued the federal government—the dam's sponsor—under Section 7 of the Endangered Species Act. However, the dam was ultimately completed after Congress exempted the project from the act's prohibitions.

The Fish and Wildlife Conservation Act

By the end of the 1970s, many legislators believed that the federal financial assistance offered to the states through the Pittman-Robertson and Dingell-Johnson acts did not go far enough in protecting fish and wildlife. Although the funds raised under the Pittman-Robertson Act supported many game and nongame birds and mammals, they were traditionally used on projects designed to enhance the populations of game species. The funds raised by the Dingell-Johnson Act were restricted for use on projects to enhance fish populations valuable in sport or recreational fishing. Thus, the states were receiving virtually no federal financial aid for projects specifically to promote nongame species of fish and wildlife.

In 1980, Congress passed the Fish and Wildlife Conservation Act, commonly referred to as the Forsythe-Chafee Act, to remedy this situation. Forsythe-Chafee is similar to both Pittman-Robertson and Dingell-Johnson in that it offers project assistance on a 75 percent federal and 25 percent state basis. However, the projects that the act will support are quite different: The 1980 act provides aid only for projects that will help in the conservation of nongame species of fish and wildlife. (By the late 1980s, there had been no direct congressional appropriation of funds under this legislation.)

Two elk graze near the headquarters of Montana's National Bison Range. The USFWS supervises the management of such wildlife refuges through its regional offices.

FOUR

Managing America's Fish and Wildlife Resources

The USFWS is a small federal agency, with approximately 6,400 employees spread throughout the country. The headquarters of the USFWS is in the Department of the Interior building in Washington, D.C., where the service's director, deputy director, and five assistant directors oversee the policy and management operations of the entire USFWS. The director is appointed by the president and confirmed by the Senate; he or she in turn appoints other high-level staff members to their positions. All other USFWS staff rise through the federal civil service, the government's hiring-and-promotion system.

The Regional Offices

Seven regional offices, each run by a regional director, are responsible for most of the day-to-day activities of the USFWS conducted throughout the country. Employees at the regional offices oversee the USFWS's extensive system of wildlife refuges, fish hatcheries, fishery assistance offices, and field offices. The regional offices are located in Portland, Oregon; Albuquerque, New Mexico; Twin Cities, Minnesota; Atlanta, Georgia; Newton Corner, Massachusetts; Denver, Colorado; and Anchorage, Alaska.

Wildlife Refuge Management

The regional offices play an active role in the management of national wildlife refuges. The offices must see to it that USFWS policy is carried out with consistency in all refuges within a specific region; provide guidance to refuge personnel on how to carry out these policies; offer technical support in managing the wildlife within the refuges; provide the refuges' operating budget; evaluate the effectiveness of the refuges in carrying out their responsibilities; and handle personnel hiring and promotion decisions. Despite the regional offices' participation in refuge management, on-site refuge personnel still retain a great deal of autonomy in determining the course that the refuge will take. Thus, the relationship between a refuge and its regional office can best be described as a partnership.

All of the states and territories, with the exception of West Virginia and American Samoa, have at least one national wildlife refuge. These refuges, 441 in all, encompass more than 91 million acres, 77 million of which are in the state of Alaska alone. The typical refuge is managed on-site or out of a nearby refuge by a manager who oversees a staff that includes a biologist, an assistant manager, and one or more outdoor education teachers, clerks, and maintenance personnel. The refuge manager reports to an area supervisor, who is responsible for all the refuges in one or more states. The supervisor, in turn, reports to the regional director. The primary responsibility of the refuge manager and his or her staff is to monitor the refuge's resident and migratory animal species and to take the necessary steps to ensure that their populations remain healthy. The refuge personnel must also oversee and regulate the public recreation, hunting, or fishing activities that are allowed on refuge land.

Refuges are not the only operational units within the USFWS for which the regional offices have management responsibilities. Other projects include fish hatcheries, fishery assistance offices, and field offices. The management role that the regional offices perform with respect to these units is often quite similar to that for refuges—for example, making hiring decisions and ensuring consistency with USFWS policy. As with the refuges, there is a close working relationship between the varied operational units and the regional offices, with the units exercising a great degree of autonomy.

Fish Hatcheries and Fishery Assistance Offices

The first national fish hatchery was established in California in 1872 for the purpose of breeding salmon. Today there are 72 national fish hatcheries spread out over 36 states, all of which help fulfill the USFWS's responsibility to replenish depleted fish populations throughout the country. Among the fish that the hatcheries produce are rainbow trout, striped bass, channel catfish, and lake trout. Closely allied with the national fish hatcheries—often sharing the same facilities—are 32 fishery assistance offices, located in 25 states. The fisheries biologists working out of these offices are responsible for distributing the fish produced by the hatcheries and evaluating the success of stocking efforts.

Field Offices

The 57 field offices, spread out through 50 states, help protect fish and wildlife habitats. These operations are broken down into three subactivities: endangered species, ecological services, and environmental contaminants. Biologists working under an endangered species subactivity aid the states in formulating their own endangered and threatened species programs and may also take direct action to promote the recovery of listed species. Staff in an ecological services subactivity provide expert advice to other federal agencies, states,

USFWS fishery workers stock a lake with fish produced at one of the service's many hatcheries.

industry, private landowners, and members of the public on how to conserve and protect fish and wildlife resources. This includes advising real estate developers on how to minimize the negative effects on fish and wildlife of construction activities and showing private landowners ways in which they can improve the natural habitat on their land. Finally, under the environmental contaminants subactivity, field specialists offer expert assistance in situations in which USFWS lands have been, or are suspected of being, contaminated by dangerous chemicals or other substances.

Research Programs

An eighth regional office, located in Washington, D.C., is responsible for overseeing the nine USFWS research centers and other research and development activities. Research is an essential activity for the USFWS, because it

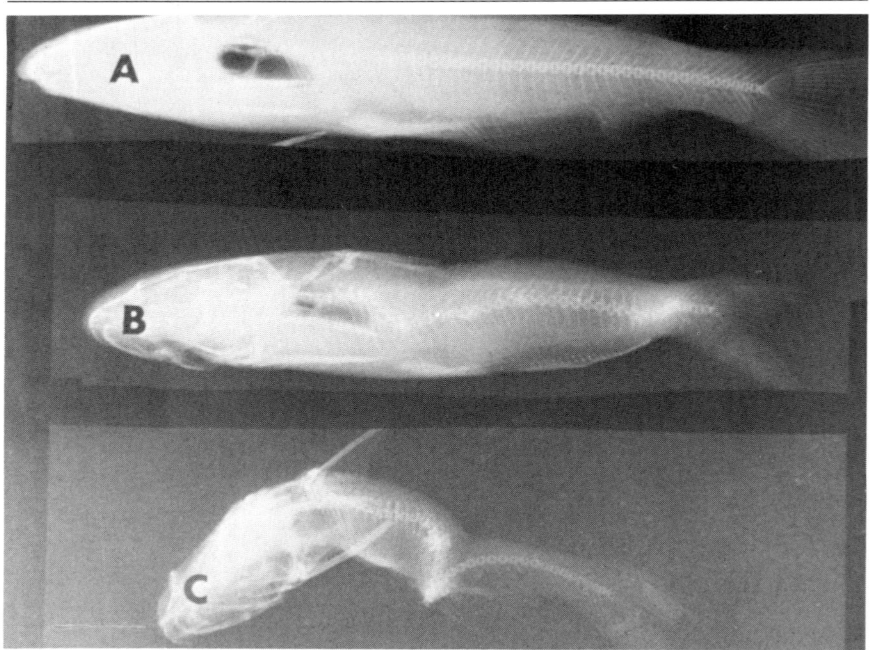

X rays of catfish show the developmental results of various levels of pesticide exposure. Such research, aimed at maintaining healthy fish populations, is supervised by an eighth USFWS regional office located in Washington, D.C.

The Patuxent Wildlife Research Center, located on 4,700 acres of forests, woodlands, and meadows in Maryland, provides surroundings for both laboratory and field research.

is research that generates much of the information upon which fish and wildlife laws and regulations are based. The largest and oldest of the service's research centers is the Patuxent Wildlife Research Center, which occupies 4,700 acres near Laurel, Maryland. The Patuxent center's research covers three broad areas: migratory birds, endangered species, and environmental contaminants.

Much of the center's environmental-contaminants research focuses on evaluating the effects of various industrial chemicals—including lead, mercury, and petroleum—on wildlife. In one experiment, researchers found that mallard ducks exposed to methyl mercury at levels similar to those found polluting the environment often experienced reproductive problems. Another experiment found that even a fraction of a drop of oil deposited on mallard eggs caused 98 percent of embryos to die. This type of information is valuable because only when researchers know how contaminants affect wildlife can they devise strategies to protect these resources. With the increasing number of man-made chemicals entering the environment there is little doubt that the center's efforts in this area will increase in the future.

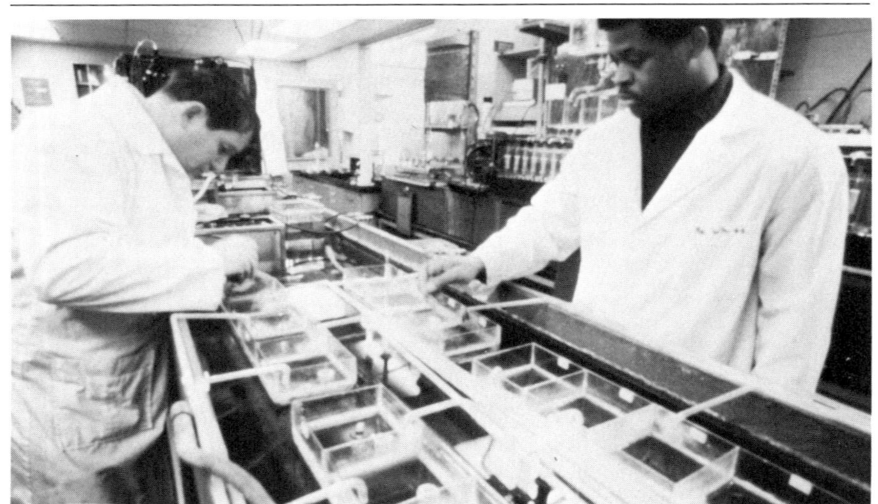

USFWS biologists conduct studies in a laboratory. The large number of biologists working for the service reflects the service's emphasis on scientific research.

Additional USFWS research is conducted by the Cooperative Fish and Wildlife Research Unit Program, which operates on the campuses of state universities in 29 states. Program personnel report directly to the regional director for research and development in Washington, D.C. As its title implies, the program is a cooperative effort involving the USFWS, the states, participating universities, and the Wildlife Management Institute (an industry-supported nonprofit conservation organization). The program's goals are to solve a broad range of fish and wildlife management problems, to produce professional resource managers at all levels of university training, to provide continuing education to employees of conservation agencies, and to make fish and wildlife information more readily available to resource managers and the public. The program has had many successes. For example, more than 20 years of research on Atlantic salmon conducted at the University of Massachusetts helped the service to reintroduce this species to several rivers in New England.

The amount of research conducted by the USFWS is quite extensive; the cooperative research units alone are usually involved in 600 or more research projects at any one time. And the agency's research efforts are continuing to grow: For example, in the late 1980s, the USFWS began construction on a forensics laboratory in Oregon that will help identify the causes of death for fish and wildlife. This type of research is useful to agency law enforcement officials who must know how an animal died before tracking down who or what caused its death.

Working for the USFWS

The USFWS headquarters, the regional offices, and the various operational units provide many opportunities for full-time employment at the USFWS. Most of these positions are filled by fishery biologists, wildlife biologists, and research biologists. There are also opportunities for ecologists, foresters, botanists, recreational planners, biological technicians, law-enforcement agents, and administrative and clerical staff. The large number of positions for biologists reflects the scientific nature of much of the service's work, such as fish and wildlife research, developing endangered-species recovery plans, and managing refuges.

In addition to the regular staff openings, there are special positions designed for college students, graduate students, and younger people. Students attending colleges with a Cooperative Fish and Wildlife Research Unit are eligible to enroll in the cooperative degree program and become service employees while going to school. To be accepted into the cooperative degree program, a

USFWS employees set out a net for a fish population survey.

student must pursue studies related to the work that he or she will be doing for the service. Upon acceptance into such a program, students are required to follow a work schedule with alternating periods of full-time work for the service and full-time study. Thus a student may spend summers and other months

Youth Conservation Corps (YCC) participants install a duck nesting box. The USFWS and the YCC provide young people with summer jobs in wildlife conservation.

during the year at a wildlife refuge and attend school the rest of the time. If, for some reason, qualified students cannot be placed directly in the permanent service work force after graduation, they still have the opportunity to apply to the service through the competitive civil service process.

There are also summer job opportunities for 15 to 18 year olds at wildlife refuges and other operational units within the service. These jobs are sponsored by the Youth Conservation Corps, which is jointly administered by the USFWS, the Forest Service, and the National Park Service. In addition to paying positions, there are also volunteer opportunities available throughout the service.

Working with Other Government Agencies

In carrying out its varied responsibilities, the USFWS has established close working relationships with other federal agencies, Congress, and state governments. The role that the service plays in these relationships ranges from consulting on resource-management issues to helping to create and enforce fish and wildlife laws.

Under the various fish and wildlife laws, the USFWS is often called upon to advise other federal agencies on issues relating to fish and wildlife management. Under the National Environmental Policy Act—landmark legislation passed in 1969 that made environmental protection a national policy—the USFWS regularly reviews all projects conducted by federal agencies to determine whether or not they will have an adverse effect upon fish or wildlife. The Sikes Act authorizes the USFWS to assist the Departments of Defense, Energy, and Agriculture in drawing up fish and wildlife management plans for the lands under their control. Finally, the Endangered Species Act requires all federal agencies to consult with the USFWS to ensure that actions they authorize, fund, or carry out do not jeopardize the existence of any endangered or threatened species or their critical habitat.

Like other federal agencies, the USFWS depends on Congress to pass the laws it will carry out and enforce. The congressional committees with primary responsibility for devising such legislation are the House Committee on Merchant Marine and Fisheries and the Senate Committee on Environment and Public Works. When considering the passage of a law that concerns the USFWS, these committees usually conduct hearings at which opposing viewpoints on the merits of the proposed law can be presented. USFWS staff members are often called upon to present testimony at such hearings.

Committee members then weigh the testimony before deciding what provisions the law should include. After passing a law, the committees then conduct oversight hearings to ensure that the laws are being properly carried out. Such hearings may result in a change in legislation or in the way the agency operates. The congressional committees may also conduct investigative hearings to better examine a particular problem facing the USFWS. The USFWS's Office of Legislative Services acts as liaison between the service and Congress, supervising and monitoring the service's role in the preparation of fish and wildlife legislation and at hearings.

The USFWS also relies on Congress for its annual budget. The budgeting process is complicated and takes nearly two years to complete. It begins with high-level meetings between the USFWS directorate and budget personnel during which various budget issues and strategies are discussed. A draft budget is developed and forwarded to the secretary of the interior, who must then consider the USFWS budget proposal in light of the proposals of the other agencies within the department, such as the National Park Service, in order to come up with an overall department budget. Once the secretary approves the entire Interior Department budget, it is sent to the president's Office of Management and Budget.

The Office of Management and Budget reviews the Interior Department's budget request and sends a *pass-back* to the secretary. The pass-back is the amount that the Office of Management and Budget will recommend that the president ask for in his budget request for the department. The secretary can appeal the pass-back if he or she finds it unsatisfactory. The final stage in the budget process begins when the president sends his budget proposal for the entire federal government to Congress, where it is considered by the House and Senate Appropriations Committees. The committees review the budget request at a series of public hearings. Finally, Congress approves an overall budget that includes the annual appropriation for the USFWS. The estimated 1988 budget for the USFWS was roughly $763 million.

Working with the States

The USFWS also works closely with individual states, which receive large amounts of financial assistance for fish and wildlife projects through both the Pittman-Robertson and Dingell-Johnson acts. In addition to financial assistance, the USFWS offers technical aid to a variety of state agencies, including those with responsibility for land-use planning, environmental protection, and fish and wildlife resources. This assistance must address specific fish and wildlife

U.S. attorney general Griffin Bell displays a jar containing a dead snail darter as he leaves the Supreme Court building in 1978. During the 1978 debate, the USFWS cited Section 7 of the Endangered Species Act in arguing against completion of Tennessee's Tellico Dam, which posed a threat to the snail darter.

resource needs. Examples of technical assistance include reviewing highway-construction projects to determine how they will affect wildlife and offering expertise on how to manage important fish populations.

Underlying the close relationship between the USFWS and the states is an ongoing debate over who owns and controls fish and wildlife resources. A series of Supreme Court cases in the 19th century was interpreted as giving states the primary authority to control and regulate fish and wildlife within their borders; by the end of the century many states felt that this authority prevented the federal government from developing fish and wildlife laws that could be applied to the states. Thus, it is not surprising that the states became concerned when, in the early part of the 20th century, the federal government began formulating wildlife legislation that was to be applied nationwide.

The states viewed the Lacey Act, the Migratory Bird Act, and the Migratory Bird Treaty Act of 1918 as examples of federal encroachment upon their traditional powers to regulate wildlife. As a result, they challenged the constitutionality of these laws. The states lost, and in a series of rulings that extend up to the present day, the Supreme Court has upheld the federal government's right to regulate wildlife. Furthermore, when federal and state wildlife laws are in conflict, federal law generally takes precedence. Despite these legal decisions, the states continue to play a major role in the management of fish and wildlife. The USFWS clarified this role in a 1983 policy statement, asserting that the states have the basic responsibility of managing the fish and wildlife resources within their borders. This responsibility, however, is usually carried out in cooperation with the USFWS.

A U.S. Fish and Wildlife Service agent exhibits confiscated wildlife products. The USFWS works alongside the U.S. Customs Service to foil smugglers of wildlife products that are banned from import or export under the Endangered Species Act.

FIVE

The USFWS Today

The roles and responsibilities of the USFWS are the product of many years of federal action designed to enhance, protect, and conserve the nation's fish and wildlife resources. Since the creation of the United States Fish Commission in 1871 and the Division of Economic Ornithology and Mammalogy in 1886, Congress has passed numerous fish-and-wildlife-related laws that established the nation's basic responsibilities with respect to these resources. In addition, various presidents have expanded or modified such responsibilities through the use of executive powers. The courts have also been instrumental in reviewing many fish and wildlife laws and helping to define how those laws should be enforced.

As a result of past congressional, presidential, and judicial actions, the USFWS has become a federal agency with a broad mandate. Specifically, the responsibilities of the USFWS fall into five categories: wildlife and fishery resources; habitat resources; federal aid; international affairs; and law enforcement.

Wildlife and Fishery Resources

The wildlife and fishery resources work of the USFWS is broken up into a number of categories, including refuge management, migratory-bird management, animal damage control, oversight of provisions of the Marine Mammal Protection Act and the Endangered Species Act, and fisheries management.

Refuge Management

The largest single responsibility of the USFWS is the management of the National Wildlife Refuge System (NWRS). Often described as the "backbone" of the service, this system is incredibly diverse, ranging from the 19-million-acre Arctic National Wildlife Refuge in Alaska to the less-than-one-acre Mille Lacs NWR in Minnesota. The breadth of species found on NWRs is also quite impressive: Of the 813 bird species recorded in the United States, more than 600 have been sighted on refuges. In addition, NWRs are home to more than 250 species of amphibians and reptiles, as well as roughly 220 species of mammals. Although the units in the NWRS are managed for a variety of wildlife species—for example, the National Bison Range in Montana is dedicated to the preservation and enhancement of the American buffalo population, whereas the Nunivak Island refuge in Alaska serves the same purpose for musk oxen—there is a distinct bias within the NWRS toward the protection of migratory birds. More than 75 percent of the nation's refuges were established primarily for such birds.

In addition to the nation's 441 wildlife refuges, the NWRS includes 152 waterfowl production areas and 58 coordination areas. The waterfowl production areas are relatively small wetlands, usually under 2,000 acres in size, that are managed to preserve habitat and provide breeding grounds for waterfowl and a variety of local wildlife. These areas are managed either by the states (under a cooperative agreement with the USFWS) or solely by the service. The coordination areas are pieces of land bought by other federal agencies and managed to preserve and protect wildlife under a cooperative agreement between the purchasing agency, the USFWS, and the state in which the land is located. The day-to-day responsibility for overseeing these areas is left to the states in accordance with USFWS-approved management plans.

Establishing an NWR: NWRs are generally established in one of four ways: executive order, statutory authority, congressional action, or donation or transfer. Theodore Roosevelt was the first president to use an executive order to establish an NWR when he created the Pelican Island refuge in 1903. Although other presidents have followed Roosevelt's lead, the use of executive orders in this manner is now quite rare. A much more common method of creating NWRs is through the use of statutory authority. There are 11 federal fish and wildlife laws that enable the secretary of the interior to establish NWRs. These include the Endangered Species Act, which provides for the establishment of refuges to protect endangered or threatened species; the Migratory Bird Conservation Act, which is used to create refuges for

The National Bison Range in Montana was established in 1909 to preserve the shrinking American buffalo population. National Wildlife Refuges vary greatly in size, habitat type, and the species of wildlife they support.

The National Wildlife Refuge System includes 152 waterfowl production areas, small wetlands that provide breeding grounds for a variety of waterfowl and wildlife. These units are managed either jointly by the states and the USFWS or by the service alone.

migratory birds; and the Fish and Wildlife Act, which allows the secretary to establish refuges necessary to conserve fish and wildlife resources.

Congress will often designate a specific area to be set aside as an NWR. The first time Congress did this was in 1905, when it created the Wichita Mountains Wildlife Refuge in Oklahoma. In 1980, Congress more than doubled the size of the NWRS by passing the Alaska National Interest Lands Conservation Act, which gave the USFWS responsibility for 16 refuges covering 76 million acres. The remaining method used to create NWRs is through the donation or transfer of land. Donations come from private groups, as in the case of the 220,000 acres that were offered by the Campbell Family Foundation for the creation of the Sevilleta NWR in New Mexico. Land transferred to the USFWS from other federal agencies can also become an NWR.

Funding Land Acquisition for NWRs: The main funding sources for the acquisition of refuge land are the Land and Water Conservation Fund and the Migratory Bird Conservation Account. The Land and Water Conservation Fund, which is supported primarily by offshore oil- and gas-leasing revenues, can be used to create almost any kind of refuge except those intended for the protection of migratory birds or waterfowl. Refuges for the latter two groups of birds are funded by the Migratory Bird Conservation Account, which is supported by duck stamp revenues.

The refuges are not the only beneficiaries of the Duck Stamp Act. Each year there is a nationwide competition in which artists submit designs for the federal duck stamp. The artist whose design is chosen does not get a prize, but he or she does retain the right to sell prints of the winning design—a right that in recent years has earned some artists more than $1 million in sales. Needless to say, the contest draws a large number of entries, usually more than 1,000.

Current Challenges to the National Wildlife Refuge System: In the 1980s, the USFWS undertook a number of initiatives to protect and maintain the National Wildlife Refuge System. In order to increase public use of refuges the service began opening more refuges to hunting and fishing, with the requirement that those activities prove compatible with the purposes for which each refuge was established. By the end of 1985, 60 percent of the refuges allowed hunting and 47 percent allowed fishing. The USFWS also initiated a project to restore refuge facilities that had deteriorated with age, called the Accelerated Maintenance and Management Program. The service took another important step

The 1988–89 federal duck stamp, by Minnesota artist Daniel Smith, depicts a lesser snow goose. Duck stamp revenues provide valuable funding for refuges to protect migratory birds and waterfowl.

when it approved a computer system to evaluate and rank proposed refuge acquisitions. By setting priorities among the proposed acquisitions, this system enabled the service to determine which parcels of land it should purchase first, given its limited funds. The service hoped that this computer system would prove useful in the future, when budget appropriations for refuge acquisition were expected to be tight.

Throughout the 1980s, the NWR system was also at the center of heated controversies over proposals to allow hunting, oil and gas drilling, and grazing on refuge lands. Such controversies revolved around the same basic question: What kinds of activities should be allowed to take place on NWRs? Although

In the late 1980s, the habitat of these caribou was threatened when the Interior Department proposed to allow oil and gas drilling inside Alaska's Arctic National Wildlife Refuge.

hunting has been allowed on refuges for quite some time, this activity has never been fully accepted by some conservation groups and others who claim that hunting is inhumane and/or incompatible with wildlife-management goals. To counter these claims, the USFWS has asserted that hunting is a legitimate form of recreation and does not have to run contrary to the goals of wildlife management. Indeed, according to the service, in cases where natural predators are gone, hunting may be the best way to control rapidly expanding wildlife populations that otherwise would run the risk of depleting their food supplies. With the service seeking to open more refuges to hunting, this debate promises to grow more intense.

As the nation's demand for energy has risen, so too have efforts to find new sources of gas and oil. One of the places where such fuel sources have been found is within some wildlife refuges. The Interior Department has allowed a limited amount of oil and gas drilling on the refuges; this activity has created conflicts similar to those encountered when hunting is allowed on such lands. Often the USFWS and conservation groups find themselves on different sides of the issue. For example, during the late 1980s there was an ongoing debate over Interior Department plans to open up 1.5 of the 19 million acres within Alaska's Arctic NWR to oil and gas drilling. Many concerned individuals and conservation organizations argued that such activity would damage valuable habitat—including breeding grounds for the nation's largest caribou herd—and therefore should not be allowed. Although it recognized the validity of these claims, the Interior Department responded that drilling would damage only a relatively small amount of land, and that the country's need for energy, in this case, outweighed the need to completely protect wildlife habitat.

The issue of grazing on wildlife refuges has also been controversial. Livestock often graze on food sources that refuge wildlife depend on; thus, excessive grazing activity can cause a decline in populations of certain wildlife species. Citing this problem and others, conservationists have fought the expansion of grazing rights on refuge lands. On the other side of this battle, however, are the ranchers who see the refuges as a valuable food source for their herds.

One of the most difficult questions facing the USFWS today is how to deal with hazardous wastes—chemical by-products generated by industry and nuclear power production. Such debris has been found at more than 40 wildlife refuges, including the Wheeler NWR in Alabama. Wheeler, visited by 600,000 tourists every year, was established in 1938 to serve as a breeding ground for a variety of wildlife and migratory birds. Between the early 1950s and 1970, the Olin Corporation manufactured DDT, a highly toxic pesticide, at a site near

Barrels of illegally dumped waste contaminate waters in Alaska's Kenai National Moose Range. The disposal of pollutants in or near wildlife refuges poses a threat to animals and their habitats.

Wheeler. Over time a large amount of DDT made its way from Olin's production site to the refuge, where it has shown up in fish tissues at levels harmful to human health. To prevent further damage from occurring, the Environmental Protection Agency and other federal agencies ordered Olin to clean up the site of contamination.

Protecting Migratory Birds

In addition to establishing and maintaining refuges, the USFWS protects migratory birds through a series of laws and international treaties. The most recent international effort in this area began on May 14, 1986, when the United States and Canada signed the North American Waterfowl Management Plan—"A Strategy for Cooperation." As its name indicates, the plan calls for cooperation in protecting the migratory waterfowl, such as ducks and geese, that inhabit both countries. One of the plan's major goals is to restore migratory waterfowl populations, many of which have declined in recent years.

The secretary of the interior is responsible for determining whether the nation's migratory waterfowl populations are increasing or decreasing. Each year, the secretary commissions the world's largest wildlife survey, in which

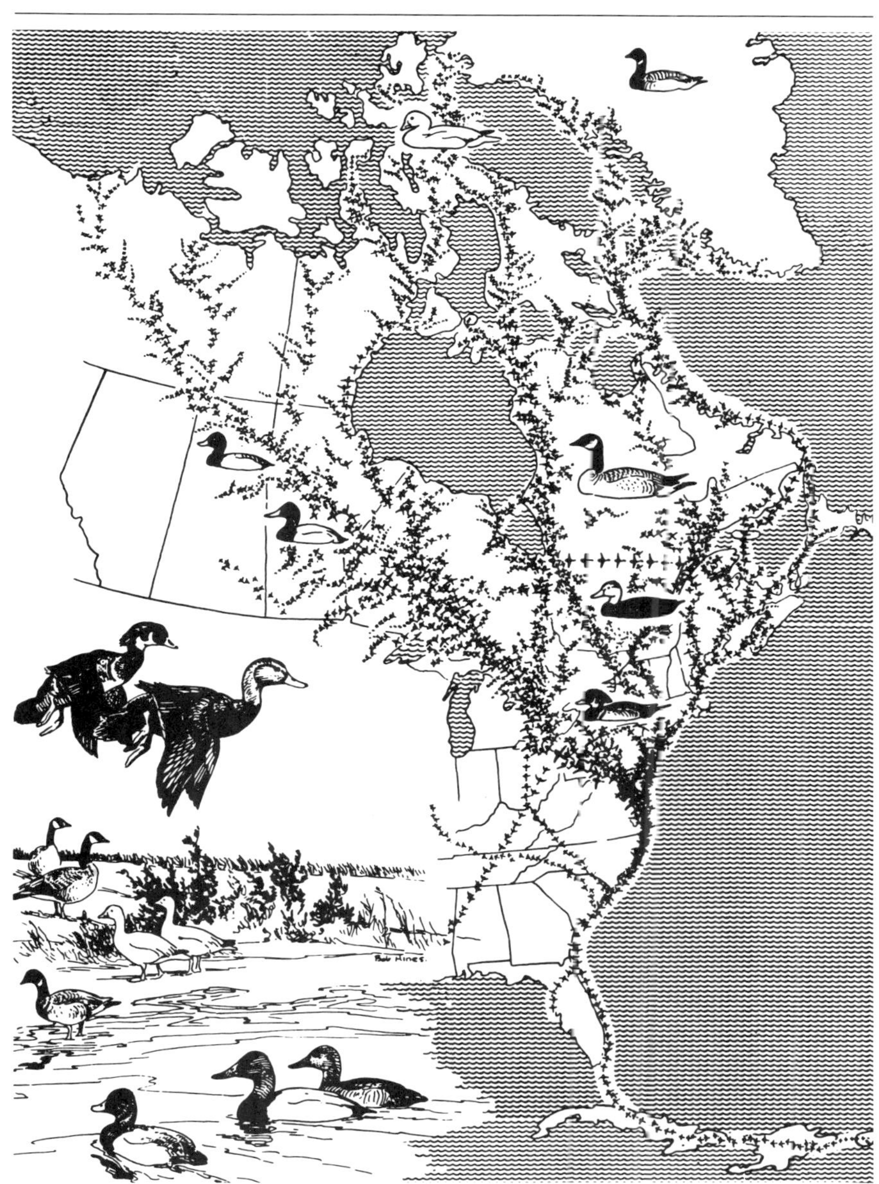

The Atlantic flyway is one of four main flyways, or migration routes, followed by North American migratory birds. The USFWS protects such birds through wildlife laws and international treaties.

pilot-biologists fly thousands of miles over nesting areas to assess the number of migratory waterfowl. Biologists on the ground conduct similar counts at various locations to check the accuracy of the numbers estimated from the air. Then the Flyway Councils, composed of state and USFWS wildlife specialists, use the results of the survey to recommend waterfowl hunting limits for each state and the length of the various hunting seasons. The secretary uses these recommendations in setting state-by-state migratory waterfowl hunting regulations that the states must then enforce.

Animal Damage Control

The USFWS has traditionally conducted extensive animal-damage-control activities on federal, state, and private lands. In 1986, the bulk of the service's

This coyote died after it attacked an animal wearing a toxic collar, a method of predator control. In 1986, most of the USFWS's traditional animal-damage-control duties were transferred to the Department of Agriculture; however, the service retained responsibility for predator control on wildlife refuge lands.

animal-damage-control program was transferred to the Department of Agriculture. As a result, the service's activities in this area today are limited to predator and rodent control on NWR lands.

Protecting Marine Mammal Populations

Since the passage of the Marine Mammal Protection Act in 1972, the USFWS has been actively involved in protecting the marine mammals under its jurisdiction—polar bears, manatees, sea otters, and other land-oriented sea animals. The service monitors marine mammal populations and ensures that the number of animals killed by Alaskan natives does not exceed that which is allowed under the act. The USFWS is also responsible for issuing permits that allow exceptions to the act's prohibition of the taking of marine mammals. For example, one permit issued in 1985 authorized a Japanese aquarium to capture and export one male and three female northern sea otters to be used in a public display.

Work Under the Endangered Species Act

Perhaps the most publicized of the USFWS's fish and wildlife resource work is that done under the Endangered Species Act. Over the years, the number of listed species has risen considerably; by 1988, there were 998 listed endangered species, of which 492 were found in the United States. In addition to those listed, several thousand species have been identified as candidates for listing. The existence of this latter group causes quite a bit of concern in Congress and at the USFWS, because candidates for listing are not subject to the protection of the act. Without such protection, members of these species may be killed, captured, bought, and sold unless some other law restricts these activities. Indeed, during congressional hearings in 1985, testimony showed that many candidate species had suffered serious population declines since gaining candidate status. By the late 1980s, Congress was considering amending the Endangered Species Act to include a provision that would enable the USFWS to better protect candidate species before they are actually listed.

Because it is difficult to keep precise records of endangered animal populations, the service cannot gauge the overall effectiveness of the Endangered Species Act. Nevertheless, most observers would agree that the act has helped to put many endangered and threatened species on the road to recovery. As of April 30, 1988, 223 recovery plans had been approved by the USFWS.

The Whooping Crane Recovery

The whooping crane is one of North America's largest birds, standing nearly five feet tall with a wingspan that can reach seven and a half feet. Much of the crane's height is in its long neck and two long, spindly legs. Snow-white with black wing tips and a red-and-black head, the whooping crane is a strikingly beautiful bird, named for the trumpetlike noise it makes; it is also a listed endangered species—one that, largely because of the efforts of the USFWS, is making a comeback.

When the first settlers arrived in North America, whooping cranes—although never an abundant species—existed in healthy populations in the continent's wetlands. However, U.S. expansion during the 19th and early 20th centuries caused a decline in the number of whooping cranes; sport hunting, specimen collection, and the conversion of nesting and feeding sites into farmland and cities reduced the population from an estimated 500 to 700 birds in 1870 to 21 by 1941. Seven years later, only 15 were left.

The remaining birds belonged to a flock that migrated between breeding grounds in northern Canada's Wood Buffalo National Park and the Gulf Coast of Texas, where the flock spent the winter—a treacherous, 2,500-mile-long journey. In 1937, recognizing the need to protect the crane's winter habitat, the Bureau of Biological Survey established the Aransas National Wildlife Refuge (NWR) in coastal Texas. The next year, the bureau began conducting aerial surveys to keep track of the flock. The Fish and Wildlife Service later established refuges along the cranes' migratory route—such as the Quivira NWR in Kansas and the Washita NWR in Oklahoma—thus

Captive whooping cranes at the Patuxent center.

providing the birds with protected rest areas.

These actions had dramatic results. The Aransas–Wood Buffalo flock grew to 59 by 1971 and to more than 100 by the late 1980s. But despite these gains the USFWS constantly feared that the flock might be destroyed by a natural disaster such as disease or a hurricane. In 1967, the year the whooping crane was placed on the endangered species list, the USFWS's Patuxent Wildlife Research Center began a captive-breeding program to ensure the survival of the species in the face of such an eventuality. Biologists removed one egg from each two-egg nest in Canada and flew the eggs to the Patuxent center, where they were hatched. (Taking one egg did not affect the productivity of the flock because, although whooping cranes usually lay two eggs, they are rarely successful in raising more than one chick.) Patuxent biologists took eggs instead of adult cranes because grown birds do not adjust well to captivity.

Developing a captive flock of whooping cranes was not easy. Patuxent biologists devised suitable diets for the birds, controlled light and temperature to simulate their natural environment, took steps to prevent the spread of parasites and disease, and prepared for any unforeseen problems that might arise. In the process of perfecting the program, the center lost many eggs, chicks, and adult birds. But despite these and other problems the captive-breeding program was a success: By the 1980s, the flock of whooping cranes at the Patuxent center numbered between 40 and 50, and there was talk of developing a second captive flock.

In 1974, the USFWS and the Canadian Wildlife Service agreed to use an unusual technique to further secure the survival of the whooping crane. USFWS biologists took whooping crane eggs from Canada and from the Patuxent center and placed them in the nests of greater sandhill cranes—a species closely related to the whooping crane that is smaller and more numerous—at Grays Lake NWR in Idaho. The USFWS hoped that the sandhill cranes would act as foster parents to the whooping crane chicks and help to create a second wild flock of whoopers. Fortunately, the technique worked: The sandhill cranes taught the whooping cranes how to find food and protect themselves from predators. The sandhills also took the whooping cranes on their annual 850-mile migration from Grays Lake NWR to the Bosque del Apache NWR, located on the Rio Grande in New Mexico—a much shorter and less difficult migration route than that followed by the Aransas–Wood Buffalo flock. By the late 1980s, the foster flock numbered around 35 birds.

Much remains to be done before the USFWS can achieve its ultimate goal of removing the whooping crane from the endangered species list. Future efforts in this area will include improving the captive-breeding program and establishing additional wild flocks. But despite the long road ahead, the USFWS can look back on its whooping crane recovery program with pride.

Steelhead trout in the raceway of Hagerman National Fish Hatchery in Idaho. Much of the USFWS's fisheries efforts involve commercially valuable fish such as these trout, which are found in the northwestern United States.

Managing Fisheries

Although not as extensive as the service's wildlife activities, the fisheries activities of the USFWS are quite important and diverse. They include the management of roughly 750 inland species, including anadromous fish when they are in fresh water. The focus of the service's fisheries activities, however, is on the 40 or so species that are important in sport and commercial fishing. To ensure that these fish populations remain healthy, the USFWS operates 72 fish hatcheries nationwide that produce more than 300 million fish per year. The fish produced at these hatcheries are then used for stocking purposes on Indian reservations and on a variety of federal lands such as the national forests.

Over the years, the USFWS has been involved in a number of projects designed to increase the populations of commercially important fish. The Mitchell Act of 1938 authorized the Bureau of Biological Survey to take the necessary actions to stem the sharp decline in the Pacific salmon and steelhead trout fisheries of the Columbia River basin. The work begun in 1938 is being continued and expanded upon today by the Columbia River Fisheries Development Program, which is run by the National Marine Fisheries Service in cooperation with the USFWS, other federal agencies, the states, and certain Indian tribes. Another commercially important species on which the USFWS has focused its energies is the striped bass, an anadromous fish found throughout the eastern seaboard from North Carolina to New England. After the population of this species declined dramatically during the 1970s, Congress requested that the USFWS and the NMFS study the problem. Their report, issued in 1984, recommended that restrictions be placed on the number of bass caught so that the population would have a chance to increase in size. Some states, including Maryland, heeded the report's findings and put limits on the number of bass allowed to be taken from their territorial waters. Work on the restoration of striped bass populations is still a priority at the USFWS and the NMFS, and both agencies continue to disseminate information on the bass and try to coax states into reducing the allowable catch of the fish by 55 percent.

Habitat Resources

Fish and wildlife must have a suitable place to live in order to survive. Therefore, the USFWS spends much of its energies on ensuring the continued viability of fish and wildlife habitat throughout the country. The service accomplishes much of this work through its dealings with other federal agencies, such as the consultation processes established under the Fish and Wildlife Coordination Act and the Endangered Species Act.

A major portion of the USFWS's habitat-protection efforts is directed toward wetlands. This habitat is essential for the survival of a wide variety of fish and wildlife, including approximately 5,000 species of plants, one-third of all the bird species nationwide, and more than half of the marine sport fish caught within the United States. Wetlands also serve other functions, such as improving water quality and protecting coastline areas from erosion and flooding.

There are approximately 299 million acres of wetland habitat in the United States, about 200 million of which are in Alaska. Of the 99 million acres of habitat in the lower 48 states, almost 95 percent are inland freshwater wetlands. The remaining five percent are coastal saltwater marshes. Unfortunately, since the early 1950s the nation has been losing valuable wetland habitat at an alarming rate of roughly 450,000 acres per year. Most of this loss is attributable to the conversion of wetlands into agricultural land used for raising crops. Construction projects have resulted in the filling in and paving over of many wetlands as well.

The USFWS is currently involved in a variety of efforts to help stem the

Most of the nation's wetlands, such as this mud flat, are located in Alaska.

Trumpeter swans in Oregon's Malheur National Wildlife Refuge. Inland freshwater wetlands such as this one constitute approximately 95 percent of all wetland habitat in the lower 48 states.

rapid decline in the nation's wetlands acreage. Since 1975, the agency has been conducting the National Wetlands Inventory, the primary goal of which is to map the nation's wetlands and to generate and distribute scientific information on their ecological characteristics. As part of this inventory work, the USFWS participates with 14 other federal agencies in a program to better evaluate the value of wetlands and the role they play in wildlife survival. The knowledge gained by this work is used by federal, state, and local agencies, as well as private parties, in developing wetland-management strategies. The USFWS also protects wetland habitats by purchasing or leasing the areas and then placing them under the management of the National Wildlife Refuge System. This is often done using funds generated by the Duck Stamp Act, which have made possible the purchase of more than 3.5 million acres of wetlands in the past 50 years. Unfortunately, despite these efforts, there is little evidence that the loss of the nation's valuable wetlands is abating.

Federal Aid

The federal government has a long history of assisting the states in managing their fish and wildlife resources. Perhaps the most important form of assistance has been the money generated by the Pittman-Robertson Act and the Dingell-Johnson Act. Together, these two acts support a wide variety of state-initiated projects designed to protect fish and wildlife resources. Projects conducted under the Pittman-Robertson Act number around 600 annually and include population surveys, hunter-education programs, and research into the effects of pollution on wildlife. More than 400 projects are conducted annually under the Dingell-Johnson Act and include habitat acquisition, population surveys, and studies on the life histories of fish. The amount of money generated by these two aid programs is impressive: Between 1939 and 1988, state fish and wildlife agencies spent $1.77 billion under the Pittman-Robertson Act, and between 1952 and 1988 the same agencies spent $873 million under the Dingell-Johnson Act.

According to most observers both the Dingell-Johnson and Pittman-Robertson programs have been extremely successful in helping the states protect and conserve their fish and wildlife. The two acts' assistance has been instrumental in increasing the populations of a variety of game animals, including deer and turkey, as well as acquiring and improving fish and wildlife habitats. For example, since the inception of the Dingell-Johnson Act more than 350 fishing lakes, covering more than 43,000 acres, were created or made

Biologists gather fish samples to test for acid rain exposure. Under the Pittman-Robertson and Dingell-Johnson Acts, the USFWS grants funds to states for fish and wildlife research projects such as this one.

healthy once again. And, as of 1983, the Pittman-Robertson Act made it possible for state agencies to stock a variety of lands with more than 1 million birds and mammals.

International Affairs

Although the USFWS's primary focus is on national fish and wildlife issues, the service is also involved in an extensive international program designed to conserve and protect fish and wildlife worldwide. The components of this program are varied and include conducting joint research projects with other countries, aiding foreign countries in managing their fish and wildlife resources, regulating certain aspects of international trade, and funding endangered species work overseas.

Through various treaties and cooperative environmental agreements, the United States and the Soviet Union work together on a wide array of fish and wildlife projects. These joint efforts include oceanographic expeditions to assess the status of various marine mammals, surveys of rare plants, and research on fish diseases. In 1986, links were established between the United States and the People's Republic of China that USFWS officials hoped would ultimately result in similar joint projects.

Over the years the USFWS has been successful in helping foreign countries better manage their fish and wildlife resources through educational and technical assistance programs. Many of the Cooperative Research Units at American universities are actively involved in international education. For example, the Alaska unit plays host to students from Scandinavian countries who come to Alaska to learn about fish and wildlife management. The USFWS's National Fisheries Center in Leetown, West Virginia, is also involved in international education, training fisheries personnel from numerous countries, including Japan, New Zealand, Scotland, and Nigeria. The service's scientific experts are frequently called upon to consult with other countries' scientists on a variety of management issues; for example, after the USFWS sent staff from the Minnesota Valley National Wildlife Refuge to Costa Rica to train workers in refuge management, the Costa Rican government was able to establish the country's first wildlife refuge.

Under the Convention on International Trade in Endangered Species of Wild Fauna and Flora, the USFWS participates in a multinational effort to regulate and restrict the international buying and selling of species threatened with extinction. The service also helps other countries protect their endangered species by offering technical and scientific assistance. One source of funds for this assistance is foreign currency: When the United States sells surplus grain to certain foreign countries whose currency, for various reasons, cannot be converted into dollars, the United States allows the funds to be spent in that country. The currency is first made available to the U.S. embassies, where it is used for building maintenance and operation. Any currency that is left over is made available to the USFWS, under Section 8 of the Endangered Species Act, for use in promoting the protection of endangered or threatened species in that country. Such funds are presently being used in Pakistan, India, and Egypt on a variety of projects, including the preparation of endangered species lists.

Law Enforcement

Many laws carried out by the USFWS contain certain prohibitions. For example, the Lacey Act declared that it is illegal to transport any bird or mammal across state lines if it is killed in violation of state laws, whereas the Endangered Species Act prohibits the taking of endangered species. If these prohibitions are to be effective they must be enforced. To accomplish this, the USFWS employs more than 150 special agents nationwide whose job is to make sure that the fish and wildlife laws are being obeyed. Each year, the USFWS investigates more than 10,000 violations of migratory bird laws alone.

Although the USFWS is responsible for enforcing a wide variety of laws, it focuses most of its energies on violations in which the violators make significant profits by breaking the law. One such instance occurred in May 1982, when two Texans were arrested for transporting 25 tons of fish into Louisiana to sell to merchants. Because the fish had been caught in violation of state law, the moment the men crossed the state line with the fish they were in violation of the Lacey Act. The two ultimately received stiff sentences, including 2 years in federal prison and state fines of more than $10,000 each.

Another area of particular concern to the USFWS is the illegal importation into the United States of species protected by a number of wildlife laws, including the Endangered Species Act. To enforce the import prohibitions written into these laws, the USFWS employs wildlife inspectors who work side by side with U.S. Customs Service agents in inspecting imported packages that could contain a protected species. It is estimated that as much as 25 percent of the international trade in wildlife is done in violation of federal laws.

Through its many programs, projects, and legal responsibilities, the USFWS benefits both the nation's wildlife and the American public. The NWRs protect wildlife species in their natural habitat and at the same time offer a natural setting in which the public may hike, hunt, fish, and enjoy scenic vistas. By administering the Endangered Species Act and other protective legislation, the service further guards fish and wildlife resources from exploitation and extinction. Through grants and technical-assistance programs, the USFWS aids state agencies, foreign countries, and private individuals in solving fish- and wildlife-related problems. And by working in concert with other federal agencies, the service ensures that government-sponsored projects do not harm wildlife resources or the habitats on which they depend.

Migratory waterfowl swimming in the wetlands of Chincoteague National Wildlife Refuge, located in Virginia and Maryland. The destruction of the nation's fish and wildlife habitats by pollution and property development will demand much of the USFWS's attention in the future.

SIX

The USFWS in the Future

Through its varied programs and activities, the USFWS plays a vitally important role in protecting fish and wildlife resources, both in the United States and throughout the world. But the service is more than a fish and wildlife organization; by protecting these valuable resources the USFWS helps to maintain the integrity of the environment, upon which human life depends.

The problems that the USFWS has faced over the years have been extremely diverse. The service has had to figure out the best way to control coyotes that prey on livestock; to restore fish populations that have been depleted as a result of human activity; and to keep endangered species from becoming extinct. In dealing with these and other problems, the USFWS has compiled a record marked with numerous success stories. Predators in many areas are now under control. Various endangered and threatened species, such as the whooping crane and the California condor, may be able to make a comeback. Valuable ecological systems, along with the fish and wildlife that inhabit them, are being preserved in refuges.

But despite these successes, there are still many problems that the USFWS has yet to solve. Hundreds of species are in grave danger of extinction. Conflicting interests hotly debate whether hunting, oil drilling, or grazing

Environmentalists warn that offshore oil rigs such as this one pose a serious potential threat to fish and coastal wildlife. Stricter regulation of such technology, they argue, is needed to safeguard the nation's wildlife resources.

should be allowed on wildlife refuges. The nation continues to lose valuable wetlands at an alarming rate. Moreover, the future promises to bring a series of worsening problems that the USFWS will have to grapple with in new and innovative ways. As the country's population expands numerically and geographically, more open land will be lost to the construction of houses, roads, and cities. Human expansion also brings increased levels of pollution; the loss of natural habitat, combined with increases in pollution, will no doubt result in the destruction of fish and wildlife populations. In addition, if present trends continue, the average American will have more leisure time in the future to enjoy nature through hiking, hunting, or fishing. This, in turn, could place additional strains on the NWRs as well as on populations of game species of fish and wildlife.

By promoting protective legislation and instituting energetic conservation efforts, the USFWS will continue to maintain the nation's fish and wildlife resources for future generations. The service's success in dealing with future challenges will help to determine the quality of the country's environment in the years to come.

The U.S. Fish and Wildlife Service

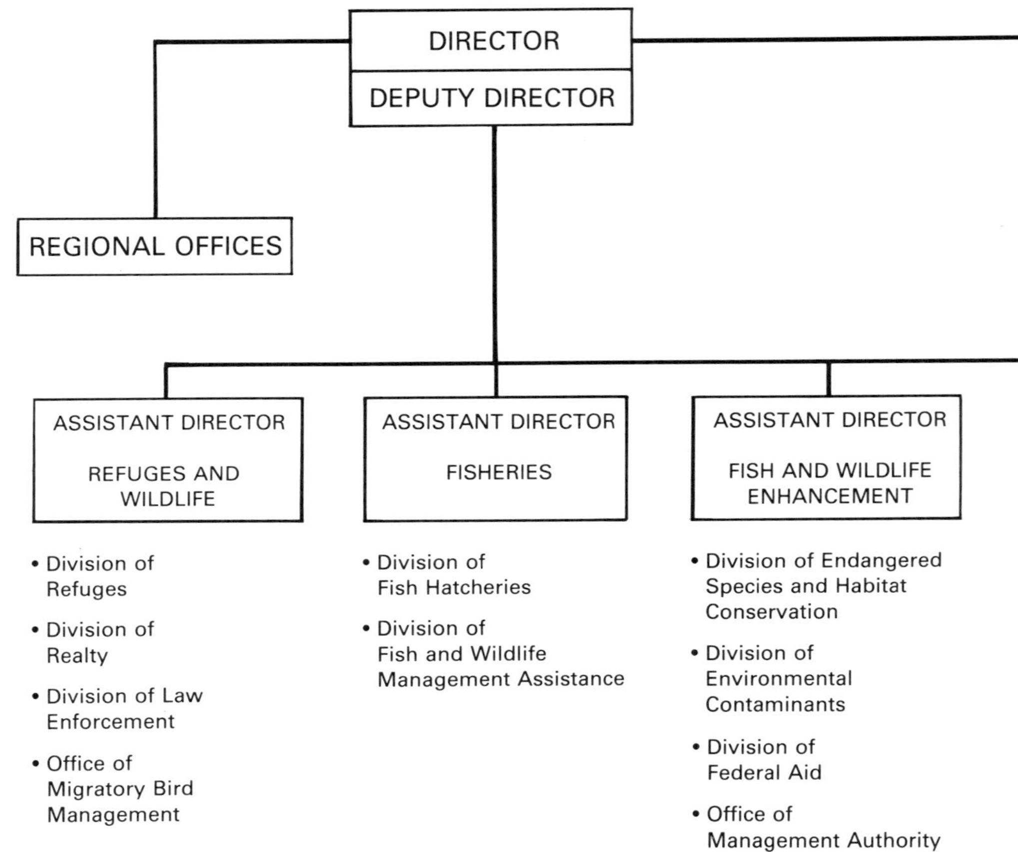

- Division of Refuges
- Division of Realty
- Division of Law Enforcement
- Office of Migratory Bird Management

- Division of Fish Hatcheries
- Division of Fish and Wildlife Management Assistance

- Division of Endangered Species and Habitat Conservation
- Division of Environmental Contaminants
- Division of Federal Aid
- Office of Management Authority

OFFICE FOR HUMAN RESOURCES

ASSISTANT DIRECTOR

POLICY, BUDGET AND ADMINISTRATION

- Division of Personnel Management
- Division of Engineering
- Division of Contracting and General Services
- Division of Budget
- Division of Information Resources Management
- Division of Policy and Directives Management
- Division of Safety, Security and Aircraft Management
- Division of Finance

ASSISTANT DIRECTOR

EXTERNAL AFFAIRS

- Office of Public Affairs
- Office of Legislative Services
- Office of International Affairs

GLOSSARY

Anadromous fish Fish that spend the majority of their lifetime in the ocean but migrate upstream to spawn in fresh water.

Botanist A specialist in the branch of biology that studies plant life.

Critical habitat Areas that are essential to the continued survival of a species.

Endangered species Existing population of a group of animals that is in danger of extinction.

Fish ladder Device that enables fish to swim around a dam.

Insectivorous Depending on insects as food.

Market hunting Hunting for profit.

Mollusks Snails, clams, or other animals with a soft, unsegmented body and either an external or internal shell.

Organic act Single piece of legislation establishing a federal agency and defining its powers.

Ornithology Branch of zoology dealing with birds.

Pesticides Poisons used to destroy insects and small animals.

Terrestrial Land-dwelling.

Wetlands Areas such as ponds, swamps, bogs, and marshes that support a variety of fish and wildlife.

SELECTED REFERENCES

Bean, Michael J. *The Evolution of National Wildlife Law.* New York: Praeger, 1983.

Brokaw, Howard P., ed. *Wildlife and America: Contributions to an Understanding of American Wildlife and its Conservation.* Washington, DC: Council on Environmental Quality, 1978.

Cameron, Jenks. *The Bureau of Biological Survey: Its History, Activities, and Organization.* The Brookings Institution, Institute for Government Research, Service Monographs of the United States Government, No. 54. Baltimore: Johns Hopkins University Press, 1929.

Clement, Fred. *The Department of the Interior.* New York: Chelsea House, 1989.

DiSilvestro, Roger L., ed. *Audubon Wildlife Report 1986.* New York: National Audubon Society, 1986.

Doherty, Jim. "Eradicate, Suppress, Destroy." *Audubon* 84 (September 1982): 100–107.

Nash, Roderick, ed. *The American Environment: Readings in the History of Conservation.* Reading, MA: Addison-Wesley, 1968.

Phillips, David, and Hugh Nash, eds. *The Condor Question: Captive or Forever Free?* San Francisco: Friends of the Earth, 1981.

Reed, Nathaniel, and Dennis Drabelle. *The United States Fish and Wildlife Service.* Boulder, CO: Westview Press, 1984.

Riley, Laura, and William Riley. *Guide to the National Wildlife Refuges.* New York: Doubleday, 1981.

Stromsem, Nancy. "Alaska—Research Challenge for the Eighties." *Fish and Wildlife News* (April–May 1981).

Udall, Stewart L. *The Quiet Crisis.* New York: Holt, Rinehart & Winston, 1963.

Whitnah, Donald R., ed. *The Greenwood Encyclopedia of American Institutions: Government Agencies.* Westport, CT: Greenwood Press, 1983.

INDEX

Eric Jay Dolin is a Ph.D. candidate in the Department of Urban Studies and Planning at the Massachusetts Institute of Technology. He holds B.A.s in both environmental studies and biology from Brown University and an M.A. in environmental studies from the Yale School of Forestry and Environmental Studies. He recently completed a summer fellowship at *Business Week* magazine and has worked as an environmental consultant for Booz-Allen & Hamilton, Inc., and as a conservation intern for the National Wildlife Federation in Washington, D.C. He has also lectured on environmental issues and published numerous articles for popular and professional journals, including *Business Week, Journal of Environmental Education and Information, Outdoor America,* and *Of Sea and Shore.*

Arthur M. Schlesinger, jr., served in the White House as special assistant to Presidents Kennedy and Johnson. He is the author of numerous acclaimed works in American history and has twice been awarded the Pulitzer Prize. He taught history at Harvard College for many years and is currently Albert Schweitzer Professor of the Humanities at the City College of New York.

PICTURE CREDITS

AP/Wide World Photos: p. 51; Library of Congress: pp. 21, 23, 27, 31, 34, 38, 44, 45, 53; National Audubon Society: p. 22; UPI/Bettmann Newsphotos: pp. 55, 77, 102; U.S. Fish and Wildlife Service: frontis, cover, pp. 14, 16, 18, 20, 25, 29, 30, 33, 36, 37, 57, 58, 60, 61, 62, 66, 69, 70, 71, 72, 73, 74, 78, 81, 82, 83, 84, 86, 87, 88, 92, 94, 95, 97, 100; Tennessee Valley Authority: p. 64